# From the Crack house to God's House

The Power of A Mother's Prayer

## Tim Francis

# From the Crack House to God's House

Copyright © 2025 Tim Francis

Published by 21st Century Press
Springfield, MO 65807

21st Century Press is a Christian publisher dedicated to publishing books that have a high standard of family values. We believe the vision for our company is to provide families and individuals with user-friendly materials that will help them in their daily lives and experiences. It is our prayer that this book will help you discover Biblical truth for your own life and help you meet the needs of others. May God richly bless you.

All rights reserved. No part of this book may be used or reproduced in any manner whatsoever or stored in any database or retrieval system without written permission except in the case of brief quotations used in critical articles and reviews. Requests for permissions should be addressed to:

21st Century Press
2131 W. Republic Rd, MB 211
Springfield MO 65807
email: lee@21stcenturypress.com

ISBN TP: 978-1-951774-44-8
ISBN Audio: 978-1-951774-45-5
ISBN Ebook: 978-1-951774-46-2

Printed in the United States of America

## Contents

Acknowlegements ........................................................................ 5
Foreword ................................................................................... 7
Introduction .............................................................................. 9
1. Breakdown to Breakthrough ............................................ 13
2. The Early Years ................................................................. 17
3. The College Years ............................................................. 25
4. Financial Freedom ............................................................ 39
5. New York City, Here I Come ........................................... 61
6. From the Bars to the Bible ............................................... 73
7. Searching for the Truth .................................................... 83
8. Signs from God – Science Tests Faith ........................... 103
9. The Worst Day of My Life ............................................. 121
10. Moving Forward ............................................................. 125
11. Mary is Calling You ....................................................... 169
12. The Ordinary Activity of the Devil .............................. 193
13. God's Solution to Fighting Evil .................................... 199
About the Author .................................................................. 225

If you like this book, send a copy to a friend or family. You can purchase more copies at:

www.sciencetestsfaith.com

francis.tim13@gmail.com

From the Crack House to God's House

# Acknowlegements

To my parents, Ed and Patricia Francis, who always showed by example the importance of never missing Mass, who could always be seen on their knees praying before bed. Thank you for your never-ending prayers and sacrifices for your kids. Thank you for pushing me to follow the facts that led me back to the source and summit of the Catholic Faith. God blessed me with GREAT parents!

To my brothers and sister who always supported me during the good and bad times of my life, especially Mike, who always believed in me more than I believed in myself.

To Fr. Mitch Pacwa & Tim Staples for coming to my house and dialoguing with my non-Catholic bible mentors. Thank you for taking the time to return emails and phone calls with your busy schedule.

To Dr. Gregory Thompson, who hosted me at so many Catholic conferences, who connected me to so many holy priests, and who pushed me for years to write this book. Thank you for being such a Godly, dedicated man for our Holy Catholic Church!

To Fr. Jim Gigliotti, who launched my ministry by bringing me to his parish and recommending me to so many priests. Thank you for being such an example of holiness and orthodoxy during these times for division both outside and inside our Church.

To Fr. Coon, who turned his obstacle of blindness into a gift from God that he shares with so many people. I treasure our friendship and your wisdom.

To Colleen Hoffman, Bill & Gayle Stock, Tom & Louise Cremona, & Tricia Smith for volunteering your time to help this mission launch. Tom, thank you for the many hours putting together the weekly devotionals that people still receive each week. Louise, thank you for writing the seven-week follow-up which untold thousands have been impacted by. Tricia, thank you for the countless hours helping make this a readable book.

To my good buddy Brian Truckenbrod, who organized and connected me to so many parishes over the years. You are a true soldier for Christ!

And most of all to my wife, Pk, and my children, Christian, Hailey, and Layton. Pk, thank for you taking this wild journey with me with these amazing kids that came from your belly. Thank you for persistently encouraging me to write a book over so many years. Christian, Hailey, and Layton, I hope we have given you many memories along with principles that will live with you long after we are gone. You don't have to believe what I believe, but you darn sure better know "specifically" why you believe what you believe, especially if it differs from the faith you have been raised in. I love you!

# Foreword

I met Tim when he came to my parish in Brunswick, Maine, to do a one-night presentation about 12 years ago. It was truly life-changing for me. As a "cradle Catholic," I immediately asked, "Why am I just now hearing these things? Why isn't this information being shouted from the rooftops?"

At the time, I had just retired from my corporate work as a trainer and motivational speaker, and I had been praying for God to "use me until He used me up," wanting nothing more than to apply whatever skills and talents I had to serve Him in whatever way He chose. I approached Tim after his presentation introduced myself, and told him I would email him a proposal.

My original idea was to partner with him and present parish presentations and retreats myself. After all, he was only one person – two of us could reach more people. I didn't hear back from Tim until many months later. He had lost my email. When he did call me, we talked for hours. Ultimately, God had different plans for me. I managed his database for several years, but more importantly, I introduced him to my son Mark, a filmmaker. To make a long story short, Mark and Tim now partner to bring important Catholic stories and messages to life on the big screen. As it turned out, God chose me to be a conduit to His much bigger plans. Was it a coincidence that I met Tim all those years ago and emailed him? Of course not. As many believe, coincidences are simply God's way of acting anonymously.

It is my distinct privilege to write the foreword to this important memoir. Tim's story is compelling. Not only does it provide critical information that all Christians should know, but it also tells of Tim's dogged determination to find the truth, to base his decisions on proven facts, and to ultimately and miraculously transition from a party-going drug addict to a devout Catholic man, husband and father with a providential purpose and devoted following. Reading his memoir, you'll laugh, you'll cry, and ultimately, you'll be inspired. Your faith will be strengthened, and you'll be deeply moved by how God works through all of his faithful believers.

—Tricia Smith

# Introduction

Everyone has a story to tell. Mine is no different from the rest, full of twists and turns, lessons learned, and moments that define who I am. As I started writing this book, I couldn't help but question myself—would I be able to stay objective? Was my story really as meaningful or compelling as others have told me? In the end, I realized it didn't matter. Reflecting on my life was a chance to grow, to learn from the past, and hopefully to move toward a future where I could be a better husband, father, speaker, and leader. I found myself asking those big, universal questions: Who am I? How did I get here? And where do I go from here?

Growing up in Ohio, I never imagined my life would turn out the way it has. Born in 1968, I was just a kid obsessed with sports and had little interest in religion. Fast forward, and I found myself battling addiction, fighting for my sanity. I've swung from being an altar boy to a party boy, from "spiritual but not religious" to being part of a non-denominational mega church, and finally back to my Catholic roots. I've danced for gay men, smoked crack with pimps and hookers, and spent hours in prayer with some of the most devout women you could ever meet.

For over ten years, my wife, Pk, encouraged me to write this book. I've given hundreds of talks about how investigating supernatural events led me back to the Catholic faith, and countless times, people have asked if I had written a book. I always brushed it off, thinking my story wasn't as powerful as others I'd read. But eventually, I gave in and decided to start journaling my journey from childhood to where I am now. I have to admit, it's a little embarrassing to see it all laid out on paper.

Later in the book, you'll meet Katya (Catalina Rivas), a woman who has received the stigmata—the wounds of Jesus Christ—more than once. She's even said to receive direct messages from Jesus for humanity. Her life before her conversion was far from saintly; she'd been married and divorced three times, living the wild life of a party girl. A famous investigative reporter once asked her, "Why would Jesus choose you?"

Her reply? "I asked the Lord that, and He said, 'If there were someone more needy, more poor, more wretched than you, I would have chosen them instead.'"

I can relate to that. I, too, fell into the depths of addiction and would describe myself as "poor and wretched." That's the only explanation I can think of for why I was chosen for the mission I've been on for the past 14 years. I was once chasing "get rich quick" schemes, addicted to crack, and always looking for my next high. Now, I travel across the U.S. sharing proof that Jesus Christ is real, present, and active in supernatural ways even today. And as you'll see in this book, much of it was driven by the prayers of my mother.

Throughout these pages, you'll find quotes from her journal and letters she wrote to me, showing the unwavering faith she had. The main reason I wrote this book is to give moms, dads, and grandparents hope—hope that their prayers are heard and acted upon, even if it takes longer than we expect. As my mom often said, "God's ways are not our ways." Sometimes, we don't get to see the fruits of our prayers in our lifetime.

Writing this book was also a way to honor my mother, a woman who never thought she deserved recognition. About eight years after she passed, I was giving a talk in Ohio when a sweet prayer lady came up to me during a break and said, "I knew your mother. We were in the same prayer group at Sacred Heart in New Carlisle." She then told me that after my mom died, the group took a vote, and they voted my mom as "most likely to be a saint."

That was my mom. Humble, kind, full of love and empathy. She would give the shirt off her back to anyone in need. The Bible says, "If I have all faith so as to remove mountains, but have not love, I am nothing." My mom lived that love every single day. She was everything to everyone who knew her.

Finally, I wrote this book for my kids. I hope they'll read it and remember the evidence for the faith they were raised in. I want them to know that my beliefs aren't based on emotion—they're grounded in evidence. This book is my way of sharing what I believe and why, and I hope it becomes something they can hold on to, long after I'm gone.

FROM THE CRACK HOUSE TO GOD'S HOUSE

# Chapter 1

# Breakdown to Breakthrough

In 2005, living in Texas, married with a family, I was invited to my friend Mike Bame's wedding in Ohio. This came about a year and a half after my mother's passing, an event that had completely shattered my world. I wouldn't claim to have loved my mother more than anyone else loves theirs, but when she died, I was utterly devastated. I felt numb and experienced a kind of pain I'd never known before. She was the heart of our family, and when she was gone, it left a void that nothing and no one could fill. So, the chance to see my family and reconnect with old college friends at the wedding was something I eagerly looked forward to. I was especially excited that my brother Paul was hosting a family get-together, bringing together all of us siblings along with our spouses and kids. I can't express how much that meant to me.

Although I had no regrets about being married to Pk and starting a family, I had countless regrets about living far from my own family, missing birthdays, sporting events, and fishing trips with Dad. Just being with them mattered so much. Yet, you wouldn't have guessed that, considering what happened after the wedding.

My college friends knew I was always up for a drink and a good time, but after college, my addictions evolved into something darker—a cocaine and crack addiction that I kept hidden. My brother Mike had an idea, as I'd confided in him back in 1997, and I suspect he shared some of it with Mom. But I doubt she, or anyone else, knew the full extent of my addiction. The wedding itself was just as fun as I'd hoped it would be. Afterward, some old college buddies wanted to revisit our old hangout spot in Reynoldsburg, Ohio, a country bar called Club Dance that was attached to a smaller place called Bourbon Street.

It's strange how sights and smells can trigger memories you haven't accessed in years. That night, I was drunk from the reception, and going back to that old bar stirred up all kinds of feelings. I'm reminded of the Kenny Chesney song, I've Been There, with its lyrics: "The devil takes your hand and says no fear, have another shot, just one more beer." I'm not making excuses, but I understand that sentiment all too well.

That's what happened that night. I can't remember the man's face, but at some point, I made a connection with someone who had access to cocaine. My memory is hazy, but I recall driving in a car with strangers and ending up at someone's house, smoking crack in a room full of dangerous people. Later, I found myself in an abandoned house with others, also lost in their addiction.

My brother Mike remembers that night better than I do. Here's how he described it:

"You disappeared after the Bame wedding and didn't show up at Paul's the next day. We called your friends but had no luck at first. I don't remember how, but eventually, someone told us how to reach you. When we did, you told us where you were. Since we were in New Carlisle, I asked Ed to pick you up and take you to his house. Dad and I jumped in the car and headed to Ed's. When we picked you up, no one said a word. I stopped at Mom's grave and told you to go see her."

By then, I was married with kids, and after my mother's death, I was determined to beat my crack addiction. But I had failed miserably. As I waited for Ed and Mike to pick me up, I felt completely hopeless. I was still in the tattered tuxedo from the wedding, filthy and reeking of alcohol and sweat. Ed later told me that when he found me, I was leaning against a telephone pole, totally out of it, in a dangerous part of town.

I knew I'd soon have to face Mike, Dad, and everyone else I had hurt—my brothers, my sister, and their family. I felt like a complete failure, and the thought of facing the people I loved most, the ones I never wanted to hurt, was unbearable. That car ride was one of the longest and most painful of my life.

As we got closer, Mike Took a detour to Moms grave site to visit Mom's grave. It wasn't a suggestion; it was an order. I was shaking as I got out of the car. Tears of shame poured down my face as I walked to her grave. I collapsed to the ground, sobbing for what felt like hours, until there were no more tears left. Kneeling in front of her gravestone, I reached out to touch the cold granite and begged for her help. I was so lost in that moment that I didn't even notice the wet grass soaking through my pants.

Mom had prayed for everyone—family, friends, even strangers. Over the years, she sensed that I was in trouble, even if she didn't know how deep my struggles ran. She prayed for me constantly. She fasted, spent hours in front of the Blessed Sacrament. The guilt I felt for causing her so much worry was crushing.

As I asked for her forgiveness, I knew she could hear me. After what felt like an eternity, I began to feel a strange sense of peace. There was a presence I couldn't quite explain. I realized I needed to fully confront my demons and change my life for good. But where to begin?

An inner voice whispered: "Start at the beginning."

FROM THE CRACK HOUSE TO GOD'S HOUSE

# Chapter 2

# The Early Years

"Dinner's almost ready; wash your hands."

"Be home before the streetlights come on."

"No swimming today, you've got a baseball game tonight."

"Come on, everyone, let's get in the car now – it's time for Mass."

What a simple life! Kids today can't even imagine a world without the internet or cell phones—just fishing, swimming, baseball games, and my gold Cimatti moped. But we loved it.

I was born in December 1968 and grew up in New Carlisle, Ohio, with four brothers and one sister. I'm the second youngest. My childhood was truly amazing. Our summers were spent at the Dip and Dive swimming pool, playing baseball games at Haddix Field, catching crawdads in Honey Creek, camping, and fishing for trout at Bass and Gravel Lakes on Wright Patterson Air Force Base. My dad worked as an airplane mechanic at Wright Pat, while my mom juggled taking care of six kids, dinner, dishes, laundry, sewing, schedules, and, of course, praying for all of us.

Dad was the disciplinarian, the hammer, while Mom was the cushion. He was a man of few words but deeply held convictions, always setting a strong example. Dad was born in Piqua, Ohio, in 1935, and raised on a farm in Russia, Ohio, as the second youngest of 11 children. Mom, on the other hand, was born in Denver, Colorado, in 1938. She was the youngest of three in her adopted family, but sadly, she didn't grow up in a loving home. Together, though, my parents were the most loving and consistent parents we could've asked for.

Our home life was full of freedom, typical for the times, and we were all extremely competitive and full of energy. I loved sports more than anything and could never sit still. I was extroverted and made friends easily, always up for a good time. Looking back, I can see how that high-energy nature got me into trouble later in life. Until about age 14, my world was all about baseball, football, basketball, spin-the-bottle at parties, and just having fun.

Our family was structured and orderly. We had dinner together every night at 5:30 PM sharp. Mass on Sundays was non-negotiable, and Sundays were always about family. One of my earliest memories is seeing my parents kneeling in prayer beside their bed every night. Camping trips, grace before meals, and attending our local Catholic church on Sundays and holy days—our lives were filled with the traditions of small-town America.

During my high school years, from 1984 to 1987, I started to push boundaries and try things I probably shouldn't have. I remember sitting with my brother Paul during my sophomore year, and he was a senior at Tecumseh High School. I told him, "Paul, I don't believe for a second that drinking a beer will make me feel any different." Famous last words. Not long after that, we were outside the Medway bowling alley, and Paul handed me a 40 oz. can of cold beer. I drank the whole thing.

"Nothing! I don't feel a thing, Paul."

"Just wait," Paul said. "Just wait."

Fast forward, I found myself waking up later, dizzy and miserable. My jeans reeked, and I quickly realized I had blacked out and vomited all over myself. "Never again!" I mumbled. "Never again!"

Of course, that promise didn't last long. I soon started drinking regularly, partying whenever I could. It wasn't unusual—most of my friends and teammates were doing the same thing.

Despite the partying, I still cared about my health. I started working out with my brother Mike when I was in elementary school, and I've worked out ever since, even during my darkest days of addiction. Back then, drinking didn't seem to cause any real problems during high school.

**SENIORS**
FRONT — Matt Yelton, Ron Christmann, Jeff Holt, Todd Morris, Darin Thatcher, Tim Francis
BACK — Mike Wilson, Bryan Finfrock, Kevin Stanley, Dan Whitt, Tony Hovan

Varsity players on my high school football team. That's me, the far left in the front row.

## Welcome to The Ohio State University

In my sophomore year of high school, my brother Mike was in his second year at Ohio State University. Paul and I had the chance to visit him, and I fell in love for the first time. Not with a person, but with Ohio State. I was immediately and completely hooked.

I decided right then to memorize Mike's social security number so I could use his ID to get into bars. Back then, in Ohio, if someone doubted the ID was yours, they'd ask for your social security number. Knowing his number was my ticket to the party scene.

That night, we went to Papa Joe's, a bar with a sign that read, "Home of the Bucket." They served beer in literal mop buckets. For $5, you and a group of friends could drink for an hour or more. It felt like Disney World for rowdy young men, and I fit right in.

I was a natural extrovert and had no problem talking to anyone, which meant every weekend at Papa Joe's, I was the one approaching girls and bringing them over to my brother's table. It was all fun and games. I was having the time of my life. By the end of the night, we found ourselves at Newport Music Hall, watching impersonators of Madonna and Michael Jackson perform. It was wild. I had my first Long Island Iced Tea that night, and I was hooked. I knew right then that I was going to Ohio State when I graduated.

## Daytona Beach Spring Break

When I was a sophomore in high school, my friend Mike Wardley told me all about spring break in Florida—white sandy beaches, oceans, and tanned, beautiful women. My brothers Mike and Paul were old enough to go to Ft. Lauderdale that year for their spring break, but I wasn't, and I hated missing out on the party. Then, out of nowhere, my buddy Tom Sawvel invited me to Florida for spring break with his family.

I remember my dad asking, "Why in the world would you want to drive all the way to Florida?"

Hmmm, let's see... did I mention the tanned girls in bathing suits? I don't remember what I told him exactly, but I was beyond excited.

But here's the catch: Instead of Daytona Beach, we went to Treasure Island, on Florida's Gulf Coast—a place more for families than rowdy teenagers. It wasn't the wild party I had been dreaming of.

## From the Crack House to God's House

Luckily, Mr. McCullum, a friend of the Sawvels, took Tom and me to Daytona for a day. When we arrived, I couldn't believe my eyes—packed balconies, crowded beaches, an all-day party atmosphere. I was in heaven. Through a coincidence, we ran into one of my brother's friends, and they took us up to the room where Mike was staying. Mike was completely wasted, holding a bottle of Jim Beam, and it wasn't even noon.

Just as the nightlife was about to kick in, Mr. McCullum said it was time to head back to Treasure Island. I tried to convince Tom to stay, but we ended up going back. I was so disappointed. Looking back now, I can't imagine what Tom's parents would've thought if Mr. McCullum had come back without us. But at the time, I didn't care about the details—I just wanted to stay at that wild party.

I remember staring out the car window as we drove away, thinking, I'll be back. Believe me, I'll be back.

### Daytona Beach Spring Break 1987

## The Early Years

**Fast forward…**

During our senior year, my friend Matt Yelton and I planned a trip to Daytona Beach. Matt was one of the first to get his own car—a Cutlass Supreme. But a week before our trip, the car broke down. Desperate to go, Matt convinced his grandfather to lend us his 1980 Ford LTD Crown Victoria, but only if Matt improved his grades. So, we asked our brainiac friend, Derek Hammonds, to hack into the school's system and change Matt's grade from an F to a B.

Unfortunately for us, Matt's dad called the school to confirm the grade, and the truth came out. But we were still determined to go, so Matt lied to his grandpa and said he was good to go. Somehow, we got away with it, for a little while. Matt got in big trouble when we got back, but it was totally worth it. We had just enough money for a week of hotel stays and drinks, and it was one of the best trips of our lives.

Chapter 3

# The College Years

### The Plan

I graduated from Tecumseh High School in 1987. To pay for college, I planned to join the Air National Guard, just like my brothers Mike and Paul had done before me. There was a waiting list to get in, so I had to wait a whole year for a spot to open up. During that year, I stayed home and worked cleaning carpets at Master Care Carpet Cleaning in Dayton, Ohio. Watching how much money the owners were making planted a seed in my mind about one day owning my own business instead of just working a job. Nearly every weekend, I drove up to Ohio State to visit my brother and my girlfriend, who was a freshman there.

### Lackland Air Force Base

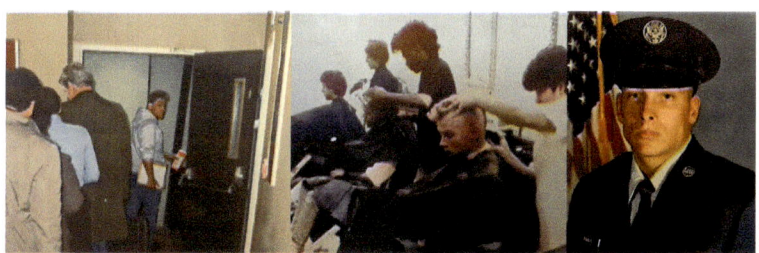

Leaving Ohio for Lackland    Getting shaved upon arrival    Graduating

Finally, a spot in the Guard opened up. They had just one position available—Power Line Specialist. During the interview, the recruiter asked me, "Mr. Francis, are you afraid of heights?" Of course, I was afraid of heights—who isn't? But I wasn't going to let that stop me, so I lied: "No, sir, I'm not afraid of heights." I would've said anything to get to Ohio State. And just like that, I was off to Lackland Air Force Base.

Before I left, my brothers had trained me to say, "Sir, Airman Francis reports as ordered, yes sir/ma'am," for any and all responses during basic training. They also warned me about the two roles to avoid: "Latrine Queen" and "Dorm Chief." The Latrine Queen was responsible for cleaning all the toilets, and the Dorm Chief was in charge of 40 men, responsible for anything that went wrong. Guess what? I was assigned as Dorm Chief!

Every day, Tech Sgt. Montalvo would ask, "Francis, do you know what your flight is eating today?"

"Sir, Airman Francis reports as ordered. No, sir. What are we eating today, sir?"

He'd smirk and say, "Russian Duck! You rush in and duck out!" Meaning we had about a minute to eat. When he tapped his foot, it was my job to tell Flight 347 they were done eating, and they had to immediately put down their silverware and stand up. A lot of guys didn't even get to eat, and if they did, it wasn't enough.

Those 30 days felt like six months. But eventually, I graduated and went on to tech training for another 11 weeks at Sheppard Air Force Base in Wichita Falls, Texas.

**Pole Jocks**

When I got to Sheppard Air Force Base, I saw these tall telephone poles and remembered that question: "Are you afraid of heights?" There were three phases to tech school. Phase I was all about seeing who had the guts to climb a 40-foot pole using just small spikes. I saw guys fall from those poles, scraping down the wood and getting pierced by sharp splinters. The instructors didn't care—they were trying to weed out the weak.

The guys who had already passed Phase I would march by and chant, "I look to the left, and what do I see? A bunch of people wishing they were me. Pole Jocks, ooh!"

Phase II was more about the technical side—learning how to attach things to the poles, like transformers and power lines. By Phase III, we were allowed to go off base, which meant drinking and flirting, and it felt like being back home again.

## The Summer of '88

Anyone who's been through basic training knows how exciting it is to get back to civilian life. Freedom feels incredible. I couldn't wait to see my girlfriend for the first time in months, to go out on the pontoon boat with my family for Father's Day, and to hit the town without worrying about getting recycled or sent to military prison. All the fun of that summer was leading up to my first year at The Ohio State University.

I was set to live with my brother Mike, his buddies Ed Bame and Greg Arnott, and two of my high school football teammates, Mike Bame and Brian Finfrock. We had a four-bedroom, three-level apartment on West 9th Street. My major? Accounting. I had never taken an accounting class in my life, but my brother Mike was majoring in it, so I figured, why not follow his lead? He was having a blast, so I thought, "If it ain't broke, don't fix it."

I wasn't exactly a deep thinker back then. I cared about doing well enough in school, but honestly, I was more focused on enjoying the college experience.

## The Ohio State University: My First Year

Fall in Ohio is the best. Sweatshirts and shorts, keg parties, football games, cookouts—it's a vibe. Papa Joe's—home of the bucket bar—was the place to be. I went to class, hit the library sometimes, worked out at Powerhouse Gym, and spent my Friday and Saturday nights on High Street. I did enough in class to pass, but the real focus was on having fun.

If you weren't in line at Papa Joe's by 10 PM, you were stuck waiting outside, unless you knew someone at the door. The goal was always to snag a table by the dance floor with a bucket of beer. The Ohio State fight song and "Hang on Sloopy" were on repeat all night, and you could always count on seeing couples making out and at least one fight breaking out on the dance floor.

Left to right: Pasquale, Mike Bame, Me, Carin, Beth, Roni, Malone

## Guard Duty and Weekend Warriors

Once a month, I had to go back home for Air National Guard duty. I never used any of the skills I learned as a Power Line Specialist. Mostly, we just changed lightbulbs around the base. I'd sneak out to my car and sleep as much as I could since I was usually hungover from Friday night. Going from the craziness of college life to this "sit around and be bored" routine was brutal.

The one constant when I was home for guard duty was going to Mass on Saturday night. Or at least, I made it look like I went. Sometimes, I'd just grab a bulletin and tell my parents I'd been there. In reality, I had no interest in sitting through Mass after a long, dull day at the base.

## Daytona Beach Spring Break

When I was a freshman, my brother Mike was a senior, and we decided to go to Daytona Beach for spring break. I couldn't wait to experience the craziness of Daytona with my brother and his friends. But at the last minute, something happened, and we ended up staying at Ormond Beach—five miles away from Daytona. I was crushed. I wanted to be right in the middle of it all.

I remember walking into Mike's room where all his friends were watching MTV's spring break coverage. I yelled, "What's wrong with you guys? We're five miles away from all of this! Let's go!" And off we went, dancing, drinking, and partying the night away. I don't even remember eating the entire week.

## The Ohio State University: The Next Few Years

After Mike graduated, I moved into a rundown apartment with my friends Ed and Mike Bame. The place looked like a broken-down Motel 6. At one point, some high school buddies came up to visit, and the electricity had been turned off. We were drinking Mad Dog 20/20 by candlelight, completely oblivious to the fact that the walls were covered in giant roaches.

We just kept drinking and headed to Papa Joe's like nothing was wrong. At that stage of life, nothing fazed me—classes, working out, and partying were all that mattered.

## Kegs & Eggs and High Street Life

Kegs & Eggs was an Ohio State tradition. Papa Joe's would close at 2 AM, but on the day of the Ohio State vs. Michigan football game, it opened again at 4 AM. There'd be a line out the door waiting to get in. It was chaos—beer slides, people on tables, buckets of beer flying everywhere. By 9 AM, we were so drunk, we'd head home, pass out for a couple of hours, shower, and then go out again before the game.

High Street was wild on Friday and Saturday nights. I got into more than my share of fights. At one point, I was even banned from Papa Joe's because we were involved in so many brawls.

Looking back, I'm embarrassed by how out of control it all was. But that was college for me, and I have to face it honestly.

I decided to stay at Ohio State that summer to work, and three incidents from that time are forever burned into my memory.

One night, as I was walking home, someone rolled down their car window and asked me for directions. After I gave them the information, I started walking away but heard them mumbling something behind the window.

"I'm sorry, what did you say?" I asked.

A voice responded, "I'll give you $50 if you let me xxxx." No need to spell it out—this guy was offering me $50 to perform a sex act on me. I was stunned. I had never been approached by a man like that before, and certainly never with an offer of money. At first, I just started laughing, thinking it had to be a joke.

Years later, I learned more about the dark, perverted world I had unknowingly brushed up against. More on that later.

Another unforgettable experience was with a guy named Maurice. He appeared to be homeless. My mom always taught me to help others whenever possible, so after buying him something to eat at Wendy's, he said he needed a place to stay. Naively, I let him crash at our apartment for about a week, feeding him and thinking I was doing a good thing. One morning, I woke up to my roommate, Mike Bame, screaming. Maurice had stolen Mike's Nike Air Jordans and cleaned out his money jar. We were broke, so every penny mattered. Mike was furious, and I was completely humiliated, feeling guilty for letting this guy in. Maurice was long gone.

About a year later, I was walking into Powerhouse Gym, and the owner, Jeff Horst, pulled me aside and asked, "Tim, do you know a guy named Maurice?" The only Maurice I could think of was the one who had ripped us off. Jeff pointed to the back of the gym, and sure enough, there he was, using my name to get into the gym for free. Jeff could see the anger on my face and asked me not to make a scene inside. I told him to send Maurice outside, saying someone was asking for him. When Maurice came around the corner and saw me, he bolted. I chased him down the street and started beating the crap out of him, right there in broad daylight. Then, a police van pulled up. They told me to get off him and informed me that he lived in a homeless shelter. At the time, I didn't even know what a shelter was.

Fast forward ten years, and I was reading the Bible. The words, "Love your enemies, do good to those who hate you. Bless those who curse you and pray for those who mistreat you," hit me like a ton of bricks. I realized I had been doing the exact opposite my whole life.

The third incident that summer was one of the wildest. I answered an ad in *The Lantern*, Ohio State's newspaper, offering $1,000 per week for physically fit individuals. I was a fitness nut, so I jumped at the opportunity, not even thinking about how hypocritical that was, considering I was wrecking my body with booze and junk food. I brought my workout buddy, Blair, to the interview. The interviewer asked me to take off my shirt and pretend like I was performing a sexual act. I couldn't believe it! I walked out, barely holding back laughter, and let Blair go in next. Blair had super fair skin, and I knew he'd be mortified. Sure enough, when he came out, his face was beet red. We laughed all the way home.

I thought we were done with that whole thing, but they contacted me again, saying they wanted me to go to Kentucky with a group of guys to dance for $500 to $1,000. I didn't even hesitate. I went to their business apartment, where about five other guys were trying on costumes. As I put my bag in the trunk of their car, one of the guys said, "Hey man, you know we're going to be dancing for guys, right?"

I was shocked. The money was tempting, but something inside me told me to get out of there. I grabbed my bag from the trunk and ran. I found a pay phone and called my girlfriend to come pick me up. The next day, my mom called me, saying she had a terrible feeling and had prayed to St. Michael the Archangel to protect me. It wasn't until years later that I told her what I had almost gotten myself into.

This was one of the first times in my life I truly experienced "The Power of a Mother's Prayer." Ten years later, on June 18, 2001, my mom wrote to me in a letter:

> "The angels are here, all around us, even though we can't see them. You, and those around you, need to be aware of that. I always remember the experience with St. Michael the Archangel when you almost went to Kentucky to dance, Tim. We have free will, and that is a hard thing sometimes."

That following year, I lived above Powerhouse Gym, right on the corner of 9th and High Street. What a blast that was! My roommate, Bill DeSantis, and I loved it. We could walk

## The College Years

downstairs to the gym, and there were no excuses for missing a workout. One night, "Big Daddy" Pasquale Caporossi came over and challenged me to a game of Tecmo Bowl on Nintendo. He had heard no one could beat me. Well, as it turned out, he never left. He literally moved in that night! Later, I found out he had left his old roommate, Bill Broughton, to figure out how to survive without electricity or water.

We also had three guys from New York living Across the hallway from us: Juice, Dave, and Jay. Juice was, without a doubt, one of the craziest guys I've ever met. Dave and Jay were powerlifters who took school seriously—Dave became a successful dentist, and Jay a high-powered corporate attorney. But Juice? He would walk down High Street in a bathrobe, completely nude underneath, and drop the robe just to get a reaction from the crowd.

One night, while walking home drunk from Papa Joe's, I got hit with billy clubs, maced, and arrested by the police in a 7-11 parking lot. All I remember is struggling to breathe. I ended up in jail with blisters on my face. I couldn't even remember what had happened—I was that drunk. Later, at Powerhouse, my gym buddies filled me in. Apparently, I had gotten into it with someone, and the cops jumped in, hitting my legs from behind and spraying me down. I probably deserved it.

On another occasion, my friends ran into Papa Joe's to tell me my brother Mike had been sucker-punched in the alley behind the bar. I ran out and saw him fighting one guy, while the other guy, a famous football player who went on to play eight seasons with the Minnesota Vikings, took off running. I chased him, and looking back, I'm probably lucky I didn't catch him. But man, did that make for a good story.

There was one more time at Papa Joe's when a huge guy from the Iowa football team elbowed me in the face. A massive brawl broke out, and I ended up in the hospital getting stitches in my head. I even urged the doctor to hurry so I could get back to Papa Joe's. I was eventually banned from there for a while because of how many fights we got into. It was embarrassing, but it was part of my college life.

### The Ohio State University: The Final Years

My last spring break at Daytona Beach nearly cost me my life. The last thing I remember that night was drinking Jim Beam. The next thing I knew, I woke up in a hospital with a blood alcohol level of 40%. That's enough to kill most people. My friend, Rob Jordan, had found me passed out in the hot tub. The fact that I didn't drown or die from alcohol poisoning is a miracle. I believe it's yet another example of the power of my mother's prayer.

I now have my mom's diary. Here's what she wrote in 1992, the same year I almost died in Daytona:

> "I have started to fast on Wednesday & Friday. Wednesdays are for our children and their special needs at a time unknown to me but not to You…. I am fearful for Tim. I know You love him, but I have to keep reminding myself that You have control of all these situations. I need to be sharing more with my children about You…"

Panama City, Florida, was my last spring break in college. Mike Bame and I brought my little brother, Phil, who was 19 at the time. What a great role model I was! We literally drove down with just $100 between the three of us. We stayed in a friend's hotel room at the Howard Johnson Hotel. Every day, we walked into a liquor store, grabbed a case of beer and a bag of ice. One of us would pay for the ice while the other walked out with the beer. We barely ate the whole week. We spent our days chugging beer, doing shots, and chasing girls. I'm incredibly ashamed to say we stole our

## The College Years

way through that week. We arrived broke and left even more broke—financially and spiritually.

That first day of our 10-day break started on the beach and ended at the pool. We didn't know the guys who started mocking me, making jokes about my size. I handed my drink to someone nearby and hit the guy square in the face. I hit him so hard he flipped backward. Phil and I fought those two guys in the sand after we got kicked out of the club. We ran back to our hotel when the cops showed up.

Every day, after stealing our beer, we'd head to the main beach area where competitions were always happening. I honestly don't remember eating much, but I'm sure we split a sub once a day just to keep ourselves going.

Each evening, we'd clean up and go out to a nice restaurant for dinner, only to "dine and dash" once we were done. We picked a different place each night, and it's a miracle we never got caught. Afterward, we'd hit one of two clubs—Club La Vela or Spinnakers—and party into the night.

### From Bad to Worse

From my mom's diary, dated January 28, 1993:

> "I am praying for Tim to find a way to make up his guard duty, get his driver's license, straighten out his VA, and keep his job and get his diploma."

In order to graduate in the spring of 1993, I had to retake an accounting class I had failed. During that time, I was working as a bouncer at Papa Joe's, and the owner asked me to come down to the basement one day. As I walked down those old, creaky steps, a man was waiting for us. That day, I was introduced to cocaine for the first time. The owner was buying coke and wanted me there to make sure the deal went smoothly, so I acted as his bodyguard.

Nick, another bouncer who was smaller than me but absolutely crazy, was there too. He used to call me "Swede" after the character in Heartbreak Ridge. After the deal was done, Nick turned to me and asked, "Swede, you want some?"

"No, I'm good," I told him. But a few days later, when it happened again, I gave in. "Sure, why not?" I said.

That was a huge mistake. Snorting cocaine gave me so much energy that I couldn't stop talking. It was an incredible high, like nothing I'd ever experienced before. Looking back, I realize that was the start of my downhill spiral.

Not long after, my roommate, Pasquale Caporossi, had some friends stay with us for the weekend. They brought "Kine Bud" from Hawaii—a high-grade type of marijuana. It was my first time trying it. One day, Pasquale asked me to toss some toothpaste down the stairs, and I threw him a pair of socks, thinking it was toothpaste. That's your brain on drugs—total unreality.

Shortly after that, I was introduced to magic mushrooms, broadly known as hallucinogenic mushrooms or shrooms. I couldn't believe that a small piece of a plant could make me hallucinate, but it did. I remember watching *Beyond the Mind's Eye* with a group of guys who were regulars with shrooms. At one point, I looked into the mirror and saw my face changing. It morphed from my dad's face, through all of my brothers, and then ended with an evil, demonic face that could have come straight out of The Exorcist.

We got hold of a Ouija board and started "communicating" with a spirit named Victor—the same name as the guy who first introduced me to marijuana. We asked Victor to show us a sign that he was there, and suddenly, the lights went out. Everyone froze in place. It scared the crap out of us. I spent the whole night staring at the ceiling, unable to sleep.

Magic mushrooms took me to a place I can't fully explain even now. They say taking shrooms opens you up to a spiritual dimension, something real and not just a hallucination—something demonic. At one point, all of us in the room saw a stuffed animal get up and start running across the room. If it had been only in my mind, how could we all have seen the same thing? Soon after, that same group introduced me to acid.

Years later, I learned that drug use serves as a shortcut to mystical experiences, and according to the book *Exorcism – The Battle Against Satan and His Demons*, habitual sin in the form of drug and alcohol abuse can be an entry point for evil. One of the most dangerous aspects of drug and alcohol abuse is how easily you end up dragging the people you care about along for the ride. It's not that you want to destroy their lives—it's more like discovering a great new restaurant or movie and then wanting to share it with your friends. You want to experience the high with the people closest to you.

The Exorcist from Indianapolis, Fr. Vincent Lampert, talks about the world, the flesh, and the devil being the main influences that lead people to habitual sin. I was caught up in the world, and I negatively influenced the people I loved. To this day, I'm ashamed that I led others toward habits that could have destroyed their lives. That guilt still lingers with me.

FROM THE CRACK HOUSE TO GOD'S HOUSE

# Chapter 4

# Financial Freedom

After graduating from Ohio State with a 2.0 GPA in accounting and no internships or job experience, the best I could manage was a temporary job at Bank One corporate. I spent my days doing the most mind-numbing tasks, like pulling staples out of papers—stuff a second grader could do. Watching my coworkers toil away in their cubicles made me realize this was not the life I wanted.

It was around that time I discovered infomercials, especially one with a guy named Don Lapre. He claimed that building residual income through newspaper ads was the key to lifetime wealth. I also bought and went through Carlton Sheets' CD program, which promised that I could quit my job and retire early through real estate. Hating my bank job, hearing all these "financial freedom" stories on TV, and my growing drug use made me a prime target for what happened next.

Feeling pressure to figure out my future, I realized I had to get serious about taking the next steps. Looking back, I should have been thinking about this way earlier, especially in college. I had been living by the motto "Carpe Diem"—seize the day. To me, that meant living for the moment because who knows if you'll be here tomorrow. I lived for fun, not realizing how much misery that mindset would bring me—and others around me.

One day, I saw a newspaper ad that really caught my attention: "HAWAII – $10k/month is what our reps average per month. International company expanding to Columbus."

I called the number, and a guy named Joe with an English accent answered. That combination of Hawaii, a $10k/month income, and an Englishman setting up shop in Columbus sounded exciting and exotic. When I showed up for the "interview," I saw a red Porsche in the parking lot with a license plate that said "Ex Cook." In Columbus, Ohio, back in 1994, seeing a car like that was rare. It immediately grabbed my attention—and looking back, that's exactly what they wanted.

Inside, about 20 people were waiting, all in suits and ties. We were told this would be a two-part interview: the first part was an informational overview, and the second part would be one-on-one. I'd never experienced anything like a "cattle call" sales pitch, so I didn't see any red flags.

A tall, gorgeous woman named Cynthia began the presentation, talking about the company, the industry, and the products. She even played a Kenny Loggins video about saving the world from environmental toxins. It was warm and fuzzy, but a little too fluffy for me. Still, I wasn't put off.

Then Cynthia introduced "Mr. K," who was a former professional chef making over $30k a month. He came in wearing a tan suit, alligator shoes, cufflinks, and a diamond Rolex—he looked like a surfer dressed up for a fancy event. He explained how residual income worked: if you could make 1% from the efforts of 100 or more people, you'd be set for life. He was smooth, articulate, and convincing. Everything he said echoed the infomercials I'd been watching. I felt like I'd found my ticket to financial freedom.

At the end of his pitch, Mr. K talked about training. "Who do you want to learn from?" he asked. "Someone who lives paycheck to paycheck, or someone who can spend a month on the golf course and still make $30k?" That was an easy question for me—I wanted to learn from the guy making $30k.

He wrapped up by asking everyone to decide if they were a "one," "two," or "three." A "one" wasn't interested. A "two" had questions. And a "three" was all in. No surprise—I was a three. I wanted to make money fast. Joe, the English guy I'd spoken to on the phone, told me and a few others to return at 8:00 AM the next morning for training.

I left feeling like I'd landed the job of a lifetime.

The next morning, I showed up for "training," but I was the only person there. Alarm bells should have gone off, but they didn't. Not for this broke, naive kid.

I was put in a room to watch VCR tapes featuring the company's owner. Years later, that guy would be banned from the direct selling industry for unethical practices, but I didn't know that then. On the tapes, he emphasized the need for training. "How much did you pay for college?" he asked. "How much money did you make during those four or five years?" He argued that if you'd invest $300 to learn from financially independent people who could teach you their methods, it was a no-brainer. That made sense to me.

So, I packed a car with friends, drove three hours, paid for a hotel, and spent $300 to attend a two-day training by a guy named Marc Accetta. By the end of the event, I was convinced I needed to buy $5,000 worth of water filters, minerals, shampoo, toothpaste, and other products. The logic was simple: "It takes money to make money. You wouldn't start a McDonald's without hamburgers and buns, would you?"

But I had a problem—I was broke. They had an answer for that, too. "How do most people pay for college?" they asked. "Loans. So, why not borrow $5k and start making money next week instead of waiting four years to graduate?" That, too, made sense to me. But where was I going to get $5k?

I decided to do something I'd never done before—ask my dad for a loan. My dad, the wisest person I know when it comes to money, grew up with 11 siblings on a farm where nothing came easy. I can still hear his sister, my Aunt Rosanne, in my head, saying, "Waste not, want not." Asking him for money to invest in what I didn't yet understand was a pyramid scheme was going to be awkward.

The training program drilled into us the idea of being a "body dragger"—just get people into the office to see a presentation, and then ask for their opinion. We were also warned that most people fail in life because they take advice from people who aren't financially independent. So, while their advice might be well-meaning, why trust someone who isn't where you want to be?

It all made sense to my 24-year-old mind.

Much of the training involved handling objections before they even came up. If someone said, "This sounds too good to be true," we were taught to respond with, "That's probably what people said when they passed on the ground floor of Microsoft or McDonald's." If someone mentioned it seemed like a pyramid scheme, we were coached to say, "Yeah, but in this case, you're on top of the pyramid." And if they asked why they had to spend money to make money, the answer was, "It takes money to make money. Name one business that didn't require capital."

The whole thing was carefully designed to address any doubts before we heard them.

Even though I tried to look at the opportunity objectively, it was hard to see the red flags. The company's pitch was simple: help people replace things they already buy—like water, vitamins, and cleaning products—with safer, better alternatives. We were taught to ask, "Who do you know who drinks water, brushes their teeth, cleans their house, and could use more energy?"

The company had celebrity endorsements from people

like Kenny Loggins and Dennis Weaver. At one point, they were even on the cover of Inc. Magazine as the fastest-growing private company in America. People were flashing checks for $5k to $100k per month.

My brother Mike and his wife, Debbie, said to me, "Tim, we tried something like this before, and it didn't work out. Tell you what—if you find success, let us know how it's going, and we'll take a second look."

That was all I needed to hear—a challenge. I made a list of everyone I knew and set a goal to bring each one of them to the office in Worthington, Ohio, to see a presentation. If they weren't interested after that, fine. But no one was escaping without seeing it first.

After a few months, I made over $20k. I'll never forget the second month's check—$10,527. It arrived at the dingy, roach-infested two-bedroom apartment I shared with my brother Phil and my buddy Mike Bame.

Feeling rich, I immediately told my brother we were moving into a three-story place with a hot tub in the basement. We were on top of the world, or so I thought.

But I had no idea that I'd end up spending more than I ever made.

My brother Mike and his wife even jumped on board. Eventually, Debbie quit her nursing job to go full-time with me at the Worthington office. Then, we made the impulsive decision to move to Toledo, Ohio, and open a 3,500 square foot office, big enough to hold 200 people. Mike quit his job at Honda, and he and Debbie sold their house to help finance the new office. We were going to be superstars in the company.

We were coached to "burn your bridges so there's no way back." The company owner said, "I was making $100k a month and didn't own a car. I was too busy building wealth."

After two months in Toledo, trying to build a team and

saturate the market with our products, nothing was working. Everything was too expensive for the local market. The stress was mounting because everyone had bought into my vision of success.

Talk about burning bridges! My sister moved up to work with us, leaving her husband two hours away. My little brother moved up with me. My college roommate, Pasquale, was putting up drywall for us. His little sister, Giovanna, even joined the business and moved to Toledo. And yet, nothing was working.

I remember hearing a tape from the company owner that said to find a market no one else was fishing in and set up shop. The #1 way we recruited people was by running ads in newspapers, just like how I was recruited. So, I went to the library and researched papers across the country. This was pre-Internet, so it was all manual. I found the Dallas Morning News and realized there were hardly any ads like ours there. Looking at the population, income levels, and market potential, I couldn't believe it—Dallas seemed perfect.

Following the advice planted in my head, I booked a one-way ticket to Dallas with no car, no place to live, and only a few thousand dollars in my bank account.

Within 60 days, I was conducting training sessions at an intercontinental hotel for hundreds of people. I wore tailored suits and lizard-skin shoes. If you'd seen me, you'd think I was wealthy. But that was what we were trained to do—"fake it until you make it," "act as if." I wasn't lying, but I had bought into the idea that temporary financial pain was necessary for long-term success.

In truth, I was one of the only people in my team consistently making money, but the cost of living and running the business in Dallas was draining what little I made. We were told, "Temporary pain for long-term pleasure." Looking back, I believe most people had good intentions. But as the saying goes, "The road to hell is paved with good intentions."

One of the nationally known leaders in my upline flew into Dallas for a training session. The goal was simple: get as many people in the room as possible and see how many would use a credit card or loan to purchase $5k worth of products. We filled the room with about 100 people and ended up with five new recruits—one at the $5k level, and the others at the $500 level.

After the training, some friends and I decided to go out for the night. One of the wild girls in the group handed me some ecstasy, or "molly." She said it would make me feel amazing, and at first, I was all for it. We hit up a popular nightclub in Dallas, and that's when I saw her—this incredibly beautiful girl across the room, surrounded by her equally gorgeous friends. I couldn't take my eyes off her. My buddy, Tim McAvoy, who's always outgoing, took the initiative to bring her over to me.

There was just one problem: the ecstasy had fully kicked in. I literally couldn't speak. Everything around me, including the tables and chairs, looked upside down. Normally, I'd have been right in my element talking to her, getting to know her. But in that moment, all I could do was stare at her like a mute idiot. She must've thought I was completely out of it, and when she walked away, I knew I'd blown it. I felt like I'd lost my ability to communicate—it was as though I had brain damage. I knew exactly what I wanted to say but couldn't get a single word out.

I've never been the type to obsess over a girl. If you ask anyone who knew me during my "girl-chasing" years, they'll tell you I'd rather grab some pizza or a gyro after the bars than go home with someone. It was always about the chase, never the catch. But for some reason, I couldn't get this girl out of my mind. Her name was Pk. After that embarrassing night, I thought I'd never see her again.

A month later, I ran into her by chance in the Dallas nightlife scene. My friends and I were at a new club that had just opened, and as we headed to the bar to grab drinks, I spotted Pk across the room with her friends. As we waited at the bar, a gorgeous blonde plopped down on my lap. I said hi and tried to be polite, but my attention was locked on Pk. I quickly excused myself, got my drink, and moved closer to where Pk and her group were hanging out.

Later, I found out that Pk had seen the whole interaction between me and the blonde. As it turned out, the blonde was her roommate. Despite that awkward situation, Pk gave her phone number to my buddy Tim, asking him to pass it along to me. Apparently, Tim explained that I had a bit too much to drink that first night, which was why I'd been acting like a zombie.

At the time, I was working with a company called Equinox International, which was launching an all-natural makeup line. It was set to be used by contestants in the Miss America pageant. Meeting Pk couldn't have been better timing. She had a whole crew of friends who were models, and I thought I could recruit her, and she'd get all her friends on board with the makeup line.

Pk winning Hawaiian Tropic

I managed to convince Pk and a few of her friends to attend one of our company overviews on a Saturday morning at 8:30 AM, followed by a training session. I was the presenter for the overview, all dressed up, looking like I had my life together. Remember, we were trained to "fake it until you make it." We weren't supposed to lie, just "act as if" we were already successful. From the outside looking in, it seemed like I was doing great financially. The reality? I was living on an air mattress with four people in a run-down one-bedroom apartment.

At some point, I went over to Pk's house to share the makeup line and the water treatment system with her. I'll never forget how dumb I felt when I showed up at her brand-new house. Meanwhile, I was living in that one-bedroom apartment with four broke people, sleeping on air mattresses with no furniture. Pk, on the other hand, had just built a beautiful two-story, three-bedroom house. The irony of talking to her about becoming financially independent was not lost on me. As it turned out, Pk wasn't interested in the products or the business. I wouldn't find out until much later that she was interested in me.

She later told me that she was impressed I didn't show interest in her gorgeous roommate, the one who had sat on my lap at the bar. Not many guys would've turned that down. She said she figured I was either gay or different and wanted to get to know me better. The only problem was I couldn't afford to date anyone. There was no way I was going to invite her to see my living situation. So, we kept in touch by phone and occasionally bumped into each other in the Dallas nightlife. As stunning as she was, I remained focused on becoming financially independent.

A Letter from Mom – November 17th, 1995:

> "Dear Tim, ... I have the feeling you are going 100 miles an hour all the time and think you can't stop to rest. I want to emphasize how important it is for you to relax your mind and refresh yourself. You can make things easier on yourself by spending time with the Lord. When we try to do things on our own without His help, we make it harder. In scripture, we are told that 'His ways are not our ways, and His thoughts are not our thoughts.'

A GREAT way to start the day is by going to morning Mass. You can't imagine the difference it makes, receiving Jesus. Always remember, it really is Jesus in the Eucharist, and making Him a part of each day brings peace, order, and direction. You also need to spend time praying for others—your family, the people you work with, and those you have problems with."

Mom was encouraging me to go to daily Mass when I wasn't even attending Sunday Mass.

Mom's Prayer Journal – February 12th, 1995:

> "I am very discouraged for Tim. I see him struggling. My concern is whether he is trusting the Lord or not. He is struggling with Equinox, and I'd like to know if the Lord is leading him. I guess I still want to fix things, or I want to see the Lord fixing things, and I don't. The way seems gloomy to me. I have to trust, and I do trust the Lord, but I don't trust that Tim understands what I've been saying to him. I am discouraged, Lord, and I don't know how to pray. I guess I think I have all the answers."

## A Turning Point

On June 7, 1996, Bill Gouldd, the owner and founder of Equinox International, was interviewed by John Stossel on 20/20. Bill warned all of us that the show would paint the company in a bad light. He told us not to watch it because it would plant negative, destructive thoughts in our heads. But I couldn't resist—I watched it right away.

After the show ended, I looked around my environment. There were four of us living in a one-bedroom apartment, sleeping on air mattresses, with no furniture. The show exposed Equinox as a pyramid scheme, revealing that most people were struggling financially. Former reps shared how the company had ruined their relationships and left them financially devastated, some even filing for bankruptcy.

At first, I tried to ignore the truth staring me in the face. I buried it deep. But after almost two years with the company, I couldn't deny it any longer. Only a handful of people were making real money, while the vast majority were losing both financially and emotionally. I had invested everything into this business, as had the people I brought in—people I loved and trusted. Coming to terms with that reality made me physically ill. I was emotionally crushed. My confidence was shattered. Saying I felt like a failure doesn't even begin to describe it. I was a broken man.

You might wonder how my family, who had followed me into the business, handled the fallout. When you face financial hardship, it can strain even the strongest relationships. We experienced every negative emotion imaginable—denial, anger, bargaining, depression, and finally, acceptance. We had moved, sold homes, taken out loans, all chasing this dream.

It would be wrong to say there were no personal repercussions. I had lost all my credibility—going from hero to zero in an instant. My brother Mike's wife still harbors some resentment, and honestly, I can't blame her. I earned that. But we've managed to put it behind us, and today, we're closer than ever.

## I'll Be Your Friend

One of my favorite country artists is Alan Jackson, and his song "Between the Devil and Me" always resonated with me. The lyrics, *"The gates of Hell swing open wide, inviting me to step inside. I'll be your friend,"* struck a deep chord, especially during this period of my life when I was at my absolute lowest. I was vulnerable, and it was as if evil itself was calling my name.

What had started in the basement of Papa Joe's came back to haunt me. Defeated, I packed my bags and moved back to Ohio. I reconnected with my old college roommate, Pasquale. He knew I had been partying with cocaine and suggested a "better" way to enjoy the high without destroying my nasal passages. Believe it or not, his intentions were good—he genuinely wanted to help. The thing is, when you're trapped in something that feels good, your natural instinct is to share that feeling with others. You want your friends to experience it too. Long-term consequences? At that age, I wasn't thinking about any of that. I had the same mindset when I introduced people to mushrooms and cocaine: Let's party together! So, Pasquale introduced me to smoking crack.

Oh, my Goodness! That first high. I can't even begin to describe it. It's like trying to explain what chocolate tastes like to someone who's never had it. Words don't do it justice. From that moment on, every time I had a buzz from drinking, my mind would laser-focus on finding crack or cocaine. Anyone who's experienced it knows exactly what I'm talking about.

At this point, Mike and his wife Debbie had moved into an apartment and started rebuilding their lives. With my tail between my legs, I moved in with them, hoping to find a decent job and get back on the right track. I managed to get hired as a recruiter for a financial services company. It wasn't my dream job by any means, but I was beyond grateful to have something steady.

That's when I met Larry Freshwater through a coworker. Larry had recently gone through a divorce and had a big house with plenty of space for a roommate. He was the life of the party—smart, charismatic, and a hit with the ladies. He looked like a GQ cover model and was making great money as a computer engineer. We hit it off immediately.

One night, after hitting the clubs, Larry asked, "Hey, you wanna go to an after-party?"

"Absolutely," I replied without hesitation. I mean, when had I ever turned down a chance to keep the party going? Moderation was a foreign concept to me.

We soon found ourselves driving into a rundown, poverty-stricken neighborhood. Larry parked the car and gestured for me to follow him. He knocked on the door of this decrepit, broken-down building. When the door opened, we were let in like regulars. I realized quickly that Larry had been here before.

The place was packed with all kinds of people. The man who opened the door gave us a look that made me uneasy—like we were fresh prey. There was a woman in a wheelchair named Della, smiling with only a few teeth left. A woman they called Body Double was dancing provocatively for anyone who would watch. And then there was Big Man, who stood at least 6'6" and acted as the drug runner, getting the goods for anyone who had the cash. Larry seemed to be the money guy in this whole setup. The entire scene felt like something out of a dark, drug-fueled movie.

This was my first time in a crack house. The alcohol I'd had earlier dulled any sense of fear or danger. I was there to smoke crack, and I didn't care who I was doing it with.

Looking back, I was beyond naive. I had no clue how much danger surrounded me. My Carpe Diem mentality—living for the moment—was still running my life, and I clearly hadn't learned a thing.

On another occasion, Larry and I were at a nightclub with some old friends. After a few hours of drinking, we looked at each other, and without saying a word, we both knew what we wanted. In the hood, they call it "The Devil's Stick." We wanted to smoke crack.

We brought our friends to the crack house—Della, Body Double, Big Man—the whole crew was there. What followed was several hours of utter madness. They had stripped my friend Tim's shirt off, and Body Double was dancing all over him in the dark while we held lighters and flashlights. The place had a revolving door of shady characters coming and going, some of whom looked like straight-up gang members. At one point, a guy sat down in front of us with a pistol, playing craps with a few others.

Body Double performed a dance for Tim, and while she did, she pickpocketed him. Then she had the nerve to ask him to pay her for the dance and the crack, knowing full well she'd already stolen all his cash. The whole situation was rigged to make us feel like we owed them money. I was convinced we were about to get robbed, or worse, shot. We bolted out of there, running through the hood until we found our car and sped off.

My life had become this tangled mess of addiction and dangerous situations. Dealers started coming to Larry's house at all hours of the night. They'd hang out, drink, play pool, smoke blunts, and drain Larry financially. Crack addiction brings paranoia like you wouldn't believe. Larry became convinced helicopters were circling his house, watching us. He'd come in, shirtless and drenched in sweat, after spending hours running through the woods behind his house. He claimed people were following him, watching us. He'd whisper that he could hear voices in the rafters.

When we smoked crack, I'd find myself glued to a window or peep hole, staring out for hours. If you've never experienced it, it sounds insane. But you literally become a slave to the drug. It owns you. I finally understood why they call the crack pipe "The Devil's Stick."

As Father Vincent Lampert, the exorcist for the Diocese of Indianapolis, often says, the devil, as God's mimic, has his own sacramentals—drugs, alcohol, pornography. Man, did I learn that the hard way!

At some point, I ended up with a guy who was shooting cocaine into his arm. We were both drunk, and he looked at me and said, "Man, you really don't want to do this."

But I was so deep into my vices by then that I ignored his warning. I shot cocaine straight into my arm. And let me tell you, it sent me to another world.

It wasn't until much later that I learned what exorcists say about our culture today—that three guiding principles open the door for the devil to take over our minds and hearts:

1. You may do as you wish.
2. No one has the right to command you.
3. You are the god of yourself.

And once again, I was hooked.

I was already defeated, but allowing my addiction to amplify those defeats felt almost unbearable. Larry and I, once athletic health nuts who loved working out, had spiraled into heavily addicted crack users, completely out of control. I vividly remember having lunch with my brother Mike, breaking down emotionally as I tried to explain just how deep I was in. I had been avoiding my family, feeling ashamed and isolated. All I wanted was to disappear to a place where no one knew me, start fresh, and maybe come back once I'd fixed myself. I told Mike I needed to go back to Dallas, Texas, to rebuild my life.

My sister had followed me to Dallas the first time, and while I returned to Ohio, she stayed. I felt like I needed to repair all the damage I had caused. She had divorced her husband and followed me on this ill-fated dream of financial freedom, and I had ruined not just her life, but many others, including my own.

Mike was trying to put his life back together after our financial disaster, and he agreed that returning to Texas, getting away from the people and habits dragging me down, might be a good move. Several years later, I received a letter from Mom that captured this period of my life perfectly:

> "The thing about bad days is—this too shall pass. Remember when you went to Dallas and wouldn't come home for Thanksgiving? That was a hard time for all of us. I've never seen Mike as upset as he was then. He called me, crying, telling me you were struggling. I'm so glad you have brothers and a sister. If you can't talk to us, you can lean on them because they really care. Remember Romans 8:28, 'All things work together for good to those who love God.' It doesn't mean the bad will disappear, but God can bring good from it if you let Him. You have to find quiet time with Him, Tim, so He can speak to your heart."

It's incredible how Mom's wisdom back then echoed similar teachings from Jesus that I would only come to understand much later.

> "It is in silence where you find Me... I do not dwell in the noise and chaos of the world. Whoever chooses silence through prayer and discipline is blessed with true wisdom, free from vanity. In silence, your soul finds nourishment. Come to Me in the quiet, in your solitude, and let My love transform you."

This quote is from "Door to Heaven" by mystic Catalina Rivas, who allegedly received direct messages from Jesus. Her words reflect the message I needed to hear at that time but was far from ready to receive.

I told Larry that if he didn't pack up and move in with his sister in California, I was going to call his parents and tell them about his addiction. He had lost almost fifty pounds, was paranoid beyond belief, and was on the verge of losing his job. I genuinely believed we were both going to die if things didn't change.

On the day we were supposed to leave—me headed for Texas, Larry for California—the drug dealers rolled up to the house, offering us big chunks of crack. Like hungry dogs fed by their master, we couldn't resist. Carpe Diem, right? Let's party!

Larry, Pasquale, and I booked a hotel, where we immediately got high. Pasquale eventually disappeared, and after what I had planned to be my "last hurrah," I left for Texas the next day. A week later, my buddy Dante Scuderi found Pasquale at the Knights Inn. He had run out of money, and Big Man (the dealer) convinced him to work for his crack supply. Death was literally knocking at his door. Thank God Scuderi found him in time.

If you've never been addicted to something as lethal as crack, this all must sound insane. Why would anyone willingly destroy their own life? I met a girl who worked for the dealer as a prostitute, exchanging sex for crack. She told me, "I hate this place so much that I love it." It sounds crazy, but that's the reality when you become a slave to addiction.

Ever wake up hungover, swearing you'll never drink that much again, only to do the same thing a week later? For a crack addict, this is a daily occurrence.

## You Can Run, But You Can't Hide

Mom's letter to me, dated October 25, 1996, said:

> "I feel like this is a time for you to turn everything over to the Lord, Tim. That doesn't mean you just sit and wait for Him to fix things. You pray like everything depends on Him, but you work like everything depends on you. Be honest in all that you do. Go to Mass when you can. When we allow Him to be in charge, He brings order to everything. I hope you're still finding comfort in your rosary. I'm sending you a booklet to guide you. I've learned that praying the rosary brings spiritual strength, especially when I'm praying for others. My prayers are heard, Tim, even if they aren't always answered the way I want. It doesn't mean there's always sunshine, but the sunny days feel brighter after the rain. When I look back, I see that in the rough times, He was always there."

Looking back, it's incredible how "tuned in" Mom was to my life, even though she didn't know the specifics of what I was going through. At the time, I thought of coincidences as just that—random. Today, I believe the old saying: "Coincidence is God's way of remaining anonymous."

I drove back to Texas from Ohio, sweating through withdrawals and determined to get clean.

When I arrived, my sister was still living with the three Pakistani guys—Faisal, Faraz, and Nabeel—who were incredibly welcoming. They were the kind of people who'd give up their bed for a stranger. I especially liked Faraz; he was innocent in so many ways, amazed by the simplest things that I took for granted, like talking to women. It was fun to go out with him and watch him try to learn how to approach American women.

One night, my old buddy Bob Jennison from Equinox told me about a nearby bar. As Alan Jackson's song "Between the Devil and Me" goes, "He calls my name, I know it's Him." Sure enough, I met a blonde who invited me to an after-hours club.

Like any addict knows, once you hit that certain point of drinking, you're no better than a dog going after a bone. I ended up in the hood, back on crack, within a week of returning to Texas—the thing I was trying to escape in Ohio.

You can run, but you can't hide.

The only positive from that night was meeting a guy who worked in oil and gas sales. He gave me his card and within a week, I had a job convincing wealthy people to invest $30,000 or more in drilling projects. The environment was like something out of Boiler Room. The sales trainer was ruthless, tearing us apart for sounding ineffective, but I found it entertaining. I was good at it and started making money quickly, so I moved into a nice apartment.

One day, I came home and found Larry sitting outside my door—the same Larry I had sent to California. He looked terrible.

"I had to get out of Compton. They came after me with a knife!" he told me.

Larry had fallen back into crack addiction in California, nearly getting killed in the process. So, he packed up and tracked me down. I was happy to see him but terrified we'd fall back into old habits.

It didn't take long. The oil and gas company had a party where someone had cocaine. Larry and I, a few drinks in, were offered a bump, and that was all it took. The moment the cocaine hit, tunnel vision set in—our entire focus became getting more. We spent the rest of the night turning that coke into crack.

I woke up devastated. It was like living Groundhog Day in the worst possible way.

Mom's Letter to me:

> "The hardest person to forgive is often yourself. When I reached a very low point in my life I turned to the Lord. I said Jesus, my life is a mess, please forgive me and take over. Think of how much you love your family and know that Jesus loves you more. Please consider beginning your healing process by going to Confession. It's a very healing Sacrament. Use the holy water every day. Bless yourself and your surroundings. Don't forget St. Michael the Archangel. Be aware of God's unconditional love. Satan knows God has a plan and Satan will continue to try to undermine the plan. You are not wrestling with flesh & blood but against principalities & powers. Talk to Jesus and tell Him how you feel and ask for help. I have been receiving strong messages from the Holy Spirit that you need to heal and let the Lord guide you one day at a time. God takes us right where we are."

To top things off, Larry and I met a guy named Mark at the pool where we were living. He was loud, outgoing, and full of energy. It didn't take long to figure out that cocaine and crack were his drugs of choice. He seemed like the ringleader at the front pool of our apartment complex. If you're addicted to drugs, you can instantly find the others like you, as if by magnetic pull. In any group, you can just sense who's on cocaine and who isn't. Cocaine doesn't care about your background—whether you come from a good family or a broken one, whether you're rich or poor, religious or atheist. It doesn't discriminate against athletes, pianists, doctors, or even CEOs.

There's an episode of 30 for 30 called "Doc & Darryl" that shows how cocaine and crack devastated the lives of two of the greatest baseball players who ever played. Then there's Lawrence Taylor, arguably the best linebacker in NFL history, who went from cocaine to crack, destroying his family along the way. If you want to understand the sheer power of "The Devil's Stick," just google "Mike Wallace Lawrence Taylor" to watch a five-minute 60 Minutes interview. It's a brutal reminder of what this drug does.

Larry and I quickly became best friends with our new party buddy, Mark. Honestly, it's hard to remember all the wild days and nights we spent at that pool. But I'll never forget watching Mark pace back and forth in his apartment, stuttering, blinds drawn, lost in paranoia. Sober, Mark was an articulate, well-groomed sales professional. But on drugs, he became a mess—like we all did. I've personally spent hours staring out of a peephole, convinced the cops were about to bust down the door. It's enough to drive anyone insane. I have a lot of empathy now for homeless people talking to themselves on the streets. Crack lures you in with that initial high and then drags you down into a dark, twisted pit of torment. When the drug finally wears off and you start to feel normal again, your brain only remembers how good that high felt. It's insane!

### Pk is back in the picture

When I left Texas for Ohio, I couldn't stop thinking about Pk. It was strange—every time I'd see "Pk" on a license plate while driving, my mind would drift back to her, this stunning, brown-eyed Texas girl. Every time I thought of her, I'd wish my life was different. I wanted to reach out but knew deep down that I couldn't bring her into the mess I was in. Now that I was back in Texas, I hoped I could get my act together and maybe—just maybe—see if she was still single. But I knew time wasn't on my side. A girl like her wouldn't stay single for long.

One night, I was out with a group of people, and everyone was taking GHB (Gamma-hydroxybutyrate), a drug that makes you feel euphoric, confident, and relaxed. Some call it "liquid ecstasy." Suddenly, I heard someone call out, "Tim Francis!" from across the room. It was Pk.

I was far from sober at that point, but there she was, the second chance I never thought I'd get, and once again, I wasn't in the right state of mind to make a decent first impression.

"You're back in Texas and didn't call me?" she asked, staring me down.

I'm sure I mumbled some short answer, probably saying we'd catch up later, but I can't even remember clearly. All I know is that I blew it—again.

After that, the group I was with decided to go to an after-party, where everyone was high on something. The next thing I remember is waking up, surrounded by people. Apparently, I had passed out and was foaming at the mouth. My new "friends" were on the verge of calling 911. Once again, it was only by "The Power of a Mother's Prayer" that I didn't die that night.

Years later, I heard a preacher on the radio ask, "What makes you think you can live like hell and go to heaven?" Boy, was I living like hell back then.

# Chapter 5

# New York City, Here I Come

I finally found the courage to reach out to Pk and invited her to meet my new pool party crew and hang out. I was growing more intrigued by her every time I thought of her. Not only was she beautiful, but she was also smart, witty, and outgoing. Her personality was absolutely infectious.

For the first time, I had met someone who could match me wit for wit. It was like a tennis match—she actually hit the ball back. After she left, Mark, our new party boy, looked at me and said, "Man, what are you waiting for?"

"I can't afford to date her right now," I said. "I need to get my act together first."

And then, naturally, we went on another crack binge. Makes perfect sense, right?

Around that time, someone in our group told us about a friend in Canada who made $10K a week doing some sort of male modeling gig. Since I was always in good shape, they suggested I could make $10K to $20K if I went to New York City for a couple of weeks. I had never been to NYC, and the idea sounded good—go to New York for two weeks and come back with $20K. It seemed like just the breathing room I needed to figure out what I was going to do to get back on track.

Of course, I didn't want to go alone. Luckily, Larry was all in. After talking to the Canadian contact, we found out we'd be modeling and hanging out with gay men. We were told nothing sexual would be required. I wasn't interested in guys, but if all I had to do was hang out with them for a couple of weeks and make $20K, it didn't sound too bad, especially since Larry would be there with me. The next step was getting accepted. We were told to send in pictures because they were looking for a wide variety of people. So, we sent ours in, and sure enough, we were both accepted.

The night before we were supposed to leave, Larry disappeared. Turns out, his girlfriend refused to let him go.

I arrived in New York City in the summer of 1997. Picture this: I got off the subway wearing cut-off jean shorts, cowboy boots, and blonde hair, looking like I just got back from Cancun with a killer tan. I couldn't have stuck out more if I tried. I made my way to 201 W 46th Street, where a woman named Denise ran the place. When I walked in, there was a glass shield with someone sitting behind it, and to the left, there was a flyer with my picture on it that said, "Welcome, Tim from Texas." It was the same picture that Pk helped me pose for and submit.

The person behind the glass greeted me warmly, "Tim! So glad to see you!" Someone came to escort me upstairs, where they put me in a small theater-like room and told me to watch a video. I figured it would be an orientation video explaining what to do next.

Instead, the video turned out to be male-on-male porn. I couldn't believe it. I was in shock. I wanted to get up and leave, but I had flown all the way to NYC, and I desperately needed the money. After the video finished, I was taken backstage to meet a group of guys, most of whom were from Canada. These guys were straight out of a magazine—shredded, male model types. The one guy I clicked with was from Boston, a guy named Todd who looked like Rambo.

I was told we'd be doing five shows a day. There were ten of us, and since I was the new guy from Texas, I'd be going on first. The idea was simple: we'd walk across the stage, and the men in the audience would decide who they wanted to "hang out" with.

But what exactly did "hanging out" mean? And where would this "hanging out" take place? The guys were tight-lipped about the details. All I knew was that they were straight guys, treating this like a business—entertaining gay men for cash. It was "just business," I kept telling myself. I was in so deep with bad decisions, I figured I'd just go through with it, make some money, and get out. At least that's what I kept telling myself.

I was "Tim from Texas" and my debut was set for 10 AM. I'm not easily embarrassed, but walking across that stage, Madonna music playing, in front of a crowd of silent gay men, was the most awkward thing I'd ever done. I could imagine dancing for a wild crowd of women, but this? This was something else entirely. When it was finally over, I was directed to a small, dark room and told to wait.

Each of the other performers went on after me, doing their routines. Once everyone was done, the men from the audience flooded the room where I was waiting. I had no idea what was supposed to happen next. Todd told me to whisper with potential customers and ask if they wanted a "private." If they said yes, I was supposed to ask where they wanted to meet up. The guys advised me to rent a cheap apartment, which would cost $200 a night, and I'd share it with other performers. But the whole thing felt off—everything was done in whispers, in secret. I later found out that Mayor Rudy Giuliani had undercover cops going into Gaiety, posing as customers, trying to catch performers soliciting money like prostitutes.

I didn't want any part of that.

Worse still, I couldn't figure out how to make any money. As the first performer, by the time I went through the motions, met people, and figured out what was going on, it was already time for the next show. I felt like a hamster in a wheel, going in circles and getting nowhere.

A couple of things from that time stand out. One day, I was walking down a busy New York street in my cut-off jean shorts and cowboy boots with an old man from Gaiety. He had asked to spend time with me. As we walked, all I could think was how ridiculous I looked—walking down the street with this old guy, on our way to a dingy apartment where he'd pay me to "hang out."

Looking back, I realize how dangerous the situation was. I could have been drugged, killed, anything. This man was married, with kids and grandkids. The whole thing felt so wrong. When we got to the apartment, I followed Todd's advice: I told the guy to put the money on the dresser. He then asked me to do things I was absolutely not okay with. We ended up just talking, and I'm pretty sure he spread the word to other potential customers that I wasn't interested in doing anything physical. I felt horrible for him—living this secret life, sneaking off to pay young men for the chance at a sexual encounter. What about his wife, his kids, his grandkids? The whole thing made me sick.

The second thing that stands out was a conversation I had with Todd. I'd been in NYC for about three days, feeling overwhelmed. Todd must have sensed it because he asked, "What's up, Tim? What's bothering you?"

"Nothing, man," I replied.

"Come on, bro, what is it?"

I didn't want to tell him what we were doing was wrong. This was his job, after all. But Todd kept pushing, so I finally said, "This is crazy, man. We're getting paid to let married men fantasize about having sex with young guys. This is not how I was raised. It's just wrong."

Todd thought for a moment and said, "What I was doing before this was wrong. I was a stockbroker, taking people's money and gambling it on probabilities, just to make a buck. People lost their hard-earned savings, and the firms didn't care. It was all greed. Here, we're not hurting anyone. We're

## New York City, Here I Come

giving people some enjoyment and getting paid for it."

I could see his point, but wow, how easy it is to justify things when money is involved. I didn't argue with him. After all, he wasn't going to quit and go home. Still, I knew deep down that what we were doing was far from harmless.

The third thing that really hit me happened about five days into my trip. Some of the performers invited me to a nightclub called Twilo, one of the biggest dance clubs in the world. It's huge—the dance floor alone is 15,000 square feet.

Before we went inside, one of the guys gave me some ecstasy. Once inside, someone offered me what I thought was cocaine, but it turned out to be something called "Special K"—a hallucinogenic drug also used as a horse tranquilizer. I wasn't expecting to hallucinate, so when it started happening, I freaked out. I was convinced the people around me were preparing to kill me. At one point, I saw a woman with snakes pouring out of her mouth, and another person's head grew to the size of an elephant. It was terrifying.

Somehow, I made it back to the apartment around noon the next day. That's when I decided I'd had enough. I booked a flight home, packed my bags, and left the next day. Once again, I had failed.

Mom's Letter to Me, October 28th 1997:

> Just a line to repeat what I said on the phone. Remember that you are involved in spiritual warfare as well as just day-to-day living. Visionaries (people receiving messages from Mary and Jesus) tell us that Satan has about reached the end of his time on earth and he is working very hard to accomplish his goal, which is for as many people as possible to go to hell. Probably one of Satan's greatest weapons is to convince people that evil doesn't exist in reality.

People think they can figure things out by themselves. Three prayers that you should be saying every morning are a morning offering, a prayer to your guardian angel and a prayer to St. Michael the Archangel. Prayers said in the presence of Jesus (In Church where Jesus is in the tabernacle) are powerful. I would suggest to you that the best way to start your day would be to go to Mass and communion. Try it and see how powerful it is to have Jesus in your heart all day. Some Churches do not open during the day have small adoration chapels that are open all the time. You cannot hear the Lord talk to you if you don't take time to be quiet and listen. Your prayers should be to ask for wisdom and guidance. That is the way to find God's will for your life.

1. Jesus, through the Immaculate Heart of Mary, I offer you my prayers, works and sufferings of this day. I offer them for all the intentions of your Sacred Heart, the intentions of the Blessed Mother, the intentions of priests and Bishops and especially the intentions of our Holy Father.

2. Angel of God, my Guardian dear, to whom God's love entrusts me here. Ever this day be at my side, to light, to guard, to rule and guide.

3. St. Michael the Archangel, defend us in battle. Be our protection against the wickedness and snares of the devil. May God rebuke him, we humbly pray, and do Thou Oh prince of the heavenly hosts cast into hell, Satan and all evil spirits who prowl about the world seeking the ruin of souls.

When I am fearful, I pray the St. Michael prayer over and over—sometimes all night long. He has been given power over Satan and his forces.

There is no magic in saying the prayers word for word. The power is in your faith. Talk to your guardian Angel. How easy it is to get off the path. Satan is very smooth and uses very sharp people to trick people. Prayer is the way to overcome this. Use your guardian angel, holy water (I hope you still have some). This is a spiritual battle. Be on your guard.

Love and Prayers,
Mom

---

Pk often hung out with our late-night party crowd, but ironically, she wasn't a partier. She wasn't doing what all her friends were doing. She owned a modeling company and was also a mortgage broker. She built her own house when she was just 24. She was the "mother hen" of the group, the "responsible one." She had no idea that addiction was threatening to destroy my life. She thought I was just a guy motivated by financial freedom, who loved to work out and stay healthy.

Of course, still using drugs, I eventually messed things up. I invited her to come out with me and the party crew from my apartment complex. We had a limo and went from club to club. As usual, after Larry and I had a few shots, we were on the hunt for our next high. It didn't take long before we connected with someone at the club who had some cocaine. After a night of drinking and dancing, everyone came back to my apartment. Pk was so tired, all she wanted to do was sleep. She'd had a few drinks and didn't want to drive home. Larry, meanwhile, was busy in another apartment turning the cocaine into crack. Pk crashed on the couch.

The next morning, she walked into my bedroom and looked at me with a mix of disappointment and disgust.

"You too?" she asked, with a tone of disdain.

The look on her face hit me like a punch in the gut. Her opinion of me meant the world, and there I was, letting her down again.

Pk had already seen so many of her friends lose their way in the Dallas party scene. I think she hoped this guy from New Carlisle, Ohio, would be different. I wanted to be different, for her and for myself, but by then, I had let drugs take over my life.

As you'll find out later in this book, a big part of my journey from the "crack house" to God's house was guided by a woman from Bolivia who receives the wounds of Christ, known as the Stigmata. Her name is Catalina Rivas, and she claims to receive direct messages from Jesus Christ. She's a well-known visionary. The addiction that was destroying my life is perfectly described by words Catalina attributes to Jesus:

> "Man continues obstinately in his bad habits, deprived of My Light, walking from guilt to guilt and losing himself because he does not take amending into account. He turns into a beast without reasoning, seeking nothing but the pleasure of his senses... He is like a vulture feeding on the fetid corpse between its claws; he would rather be hunted than leave the prey. The soul accustomed to vice commits the same sin over and over, even at the moment of death. If a person is assaulted by a wicked man, he is not rendered unable to defend himself at the first blow. But if he receives two or three wounds afterward, he will lose strength and die. It is the same for the soul. The first and second time, it still has the strength to resist, but if it continues to sin, the enemy attacks it and strips it of all strength to

resist. A bad habit turns into a need to sin, as man becomes a slave to that passion. In the end, he makes peace with sin."

Reading these words reminded me of what Paul said in Romans 6:16: "Do you not know that if you present yourselves to someone as obedient slaves, you are slaves of the one you obey, either of sin, which leads to death, or of obedience, which leads to righteousness?"

When Pk realized I was caught in this web of vice—deception, division, and destruction—she didn't run. Instead, she wanted to help. She saw something in me that gave her hope for what I could become. At that point in my life, three women stood "between the Devil and me"—Mary, the mother of God; my own mother; and Pk.

My relationship with Pk grew from a simple friendship into something more. We both wanted to build a strong relationship, so we read books and attended conferences that taught communication techniques for couples. We learned how to write "love letters," a way of communicating that helps love and understanding rise above anger and resentment in times of turmoil. Honestly, without this "love letter" technique, we probably wouldn't be married today. We'll have been married for 25 years as of August 12th, 2024.

After a few months of the party merry-go-round, Pk invited me to move into her house to help me get away from the wrong influences. Around the same time, I reconnected with Cindy, an old friend from my Equinox days. Like many of us who had chased the "financial freedom" dream and were now recovering from broken dreams and relationships, she was working for a company selling windows. I gave it a try for a while, but it didn't take long for me to get sick of the smoke and mirrors involved in manipulating low-income people to finance overpriced windows, just so we could make commissions. Once again, I was using my sales and persuasion skills in a way that didn't feel right. I needed something real, something worthwhile, something I could be proud of.

Cindy introduced me to her boyfriend, Rob, who was starting a company designed to help people find legitimate work-from-home opportunities. I was asked to head up the direct mail program that targeted people looking for home-based businesses. Pk and I became very close with Rob and Cindy. We were inseparable—sharing books, communication techniques, and spending every weekend together. Pk started working with Cindy, and I worked with Rob. But after a while, Rob and Cindy started pulling away, becoming busy and unavailable. They didn't push it on us, but they invited us a few times to visit their new church. It always seemed like we couldn't make it after being out late at the bars on weekends.

Finally, Pk made it a point to get us up early one Sunday to check out their new church. It was a non-denominational mega-church called Fellowship Church in Grapevine, TX, and it was amazing. Their messages seemed to speak directly to us, and the services were filled with creativity and entertainment. It was like a top-notch concert or play, and it was all about Jesus. The church was massive, with an average weekly attendance of over 24,000 people. The pastor spoke from a raised platform with large screens, so no one missed a thing. The live Christian music blared from the speakers, and everyone dressed in a hip, modern way. These weren't the kind of churchgoers I had pictured. We felt like we'd found our tribe.

Once again, I moved away from the party crowd. Rob and I worked out together, worked together, and eventually started praying and reading the Bible together every day. Pk's income had taken a hit, but fortunately, I was making enough to cover the bills. It felt great—a new relationship, new friends, a new job. Had I finally turned the corner?

Letter From Mom May 1998:

> I think of you often and wonder how you are and what is going on. Of course you are always in my prayers. I hope you are going to Mass. It's not for my benefit but for yours. I know because of my own experience in life that Jesus gives a piece of His heart that no one can take away. Praying before the Blessed Sacrament is very important. I am not talking about praying for "things" but for guidance in all parts of life. One thing you must always remember is that the Lord will never bless anything dishonest. It may be successful for a while, but it won't be the right success. The devil "blesses" some very evil things with the success of the world. People sell their souls for money, fame, & power. Success doesn't necessarily mean getting rich. I pray you will ask the Lord's guidance an ask Him to show you the way.

Ironically, I now promote a book called *My Human Heart* that promotes the value of the Eucharist in the Mass.

## Chapter 6

# From the Bars to the Bible

Pk and I grew incredibly close and soon became inseparable. We both loved to read and sought out insights and knowledge wherever we could. We were also both very health-conscious, and we enjoyed the Dallas-Fort Worth nightlife. I even brought Pk home to the Francis family reunion. Despite a few arguments, which we worked through using the "love letter" technique, we were convinced that we were soulmates. We complemented each other well. I was the spontaneous, "big picture" kind of guy, and she was the "let's not jump into things—small details, plan it out, and think long-term" kind of girl.

Growing up in New Carlisle, Ohio, I went to a small Catholic church and, to be honest, found it pretty boring. But this mega-church environment we found in Texas was a completely different experience—so welcoming and energizing. We were immediately drawn into a network of friendly people who were in a similar stage of life. I was asked to be part of a men's group that met weekly, and since I was already working with Rob, we were reading the Bible daily and working out during lunch. At the same time, we were invited to attend a Wednesday night event called Metro Bible Study with Pastor Tommy Nelson. We had never seen anything like it. Hundreds of people, many of them our age or younger, all with their Bibles open, hands raised in genuine worship. People were pouring their minds and hearts into this Wednesday night study.

Tommy Nelson, the preacher, was a former quarterback at North Texas, a real "man's man." He spoke with authority and strength, captivating the room without being sensational. I was drawn to his focus on virtues and values, especially on how to be a great husband and father. Over time, I started listening to Christian radio and constantly tuned in to people like Dr. David Jeremiah, Chuck Swindoll, Charles Stanley, Ed Young, Hank Hanegraaff, Tony Evans, John MacArthur, and Allistair Begg, among others.

Pk and I seemed to go from the "bar scene" to the "Bible scene" almost overnight. I remember reading the Bible for the first time and nearly falling out of my chair when I came across this passage:

> "Do not be deceived: Neither the sexually immoral nor idolaters nor adulterers nor men who have sex with men nor thieves nor the greedy nor drunkards nor slanderers nor swindlers will inherit the kingdom of God" (1 Corinthians 6:9-10).

I couldn't believe what I was reading. Somewhere along the way, in my youth, I must have heard that sex before marriage and getting drunk were wrong, but those things were such a normal part of college life in my twenties that I never gave it a second thought. It was just what everyone did.

Then we were told that living together before marriage wasn't right. So, I moved out and into Rob's apartment. I was also told that I shouldn't be drinking anymore because I might cause someone else to stumble. They showed me Romans 14:21: "It is good not to eat meat or drink wine or do anything that causes your brother to stumble."

We wanted to do things the right way, so I gave up alcohol. Honestly, this was completely foreign to me. The idea of not having a beer at a football game was like eating spaghetti with your hands instead of a fork and knife! Looking back, given my history with alcohol leading me to drugs, it probably made sense for me to give it up. But in normal circumstances, I don't think giving up every social habit is necessary just because someone else might struggle with it. If you're out to eat with someone who's a recovering alcoholic, sure, don't drink—but applying that Bible verse to every possible situation seems a little extreme to me now.

Pk and I were deeply in love. Moving to Texas and starting a family wasn't originally part of my plan, but once we fell in love, started doing everything together, and began this new life built on Christian principles, proposing to her seemed like the most natural thing in the world. And, thankfully, she said yes!

We took pre-marriage classes at Fellowship Church. Since I was raised Catholic, I thought we should get married in a Catholic church. But when we met with the deacon at the Catholic Cathedral in Dallas, he informed us we'd have to sign a paper promising to raise our kids Catholic. Since we weren't even attending a Catholic church, that didn't feel right. As Pk planned the wedding, obstacles seemed to pop up around every corner, especially with trying to accommodate family and friends—most of mine from Ohio and hers from Texas. It became a three-ring circus trying to juggle everything. In the end, we felt that marriage was about the two of us, so we decided to have a private ceremony in Lake Tahoe.

My mom and dad were disappointed that we weren't getting married in a Catholic church. Years later, I found out my mom had to talk my dad into even coming. It was extremely hard for them to support a wedding outside the Catholic faith. Mom told Pk she wasn't happy about it, but she made an exception because she knew we were genuinely seeking God and truth.

From the Crack House to God's House

Left to right—Dad, Mom, Me, Pk, Gaye (Pk's Mom) & Lynn (Pk's stepdad)

The day after our wedding in Lake Tahoe

## Mom and Dad Come to Texas

My little brother Phil followed in the family tradition and joined the Air National Guard, just like Mike, Paul, and I had. He was stationed in Wichita Falls, Texas for training, which worked out perfectly, as he got a weekend off just as my mom and dad had planned a visit to see Pk and me.

My sister Debbie had also followed me to Texas during my first stint here for business. Naturally, we invited her to join us at Fellowship Church. I recently asked her to reflect on her first impressions of the church. She responded with a bit of irony, saying, "It was different because it's not Church. It's more like a place where people go to say hi and watch a performance."

We also invited my mom and dad to attend a service with us. It was difficult for them, but they agreed to come. My dad, ever the straightforward, blue-collar man, said after the service, "Well, who wouldn't come to this? You get free lemonade, cookies, and a free concert with comfy seats!"

Dad, Mom, Debbie, Phil, Pk, and me at lunch after attending church

My dad judged it as entertainment. I remember thinking, "What's wrong with entertainment if it gets people to follow Jesus?"

The pastor at Fellowship Church often said Jesus was a great entertainer. He took pride in the creativity of their services. They even had a yearly C3 Conference, where leaders from around the world came to discuss creativity in the church. To me, it made sense—using entertainment to capture people's attention, so they could learn about Christ.

But because of my past experiences with Equinox, I had concerns. In Equinox, everything was about making people feel welcomed and inspired, and I started seeing similarities. My red flags went up, as I worried that too many people were getting swept up in the emotion of it all, just like in Equinox. People in tghe Equinox twisted Scripture to fit their narrative, so I had to be vigilant about seeking the real, unfiltered truth.

At one point, Pk and I were attending both Catholic Mass and services at Fellowship Church. Our son, Christian, would ask, "Are we going to the fun church or the boring church, Dad?" Today, at 23, Christian prefers the Latin Mass. He even refuses to use comfortable kneelers, saying, "Why should we be comfortable when Jesus hung on the cross for us?" More on that later...

My mom would often remind me, "Tim, without a priest, you have no Mass. Without the Mass, you have no Eucharist—the body, blood, soul, and divinity of Jesus. Jesus said, 'This is My body, this is My blood. If you eat My flesh and drink My blood, you will have eternal life.' I want you and your family to have eternal life. I'm sure Jesus is present at Fellowship Church 'spiritually,' but He is not there physically."

Mom's Letter, July 1999:

> I can't imagine what it would be like not to have the Eucharist. I can't imagine what it would be like if I didn't know Jesus was present in the Eucharist and I didn't know I could spend special time of prayer in front of the Blessed Sacrament and realize His presence there. God made us the way we are, we are both spirit and human. His Church meets all the needs of what He created. He touches us in a special way in the Sacraments (7 of them) and he comes to us physically in the Eucharist. There is a booklet I left you called *"Pillar of Fire, Pillar of Truth."* It is a book about the Church and what we believe. Jesus left His Church on the earth; God does not do incomplete things. What I learned about Protestant Churches over the years is that they all have part of the truth. Because some person decided they felt a certain way and they believed a certain way that is what they believe, until someone disagrees—then they start their own Church. I was in a Protestant Church about five years ago for a funeral and it really hit me, they don't have the tabernacle. They have the spirit of Jesus, but they don't have His real presence. You have been given special gifts and it's your job to find out what the Lord wants you to do. If you want to know the truth, you need to spend some time with the Lord. If you can't find a Catholic Church that has Adoration of the Blessed Sacrament or Benediction, go to weekday Mass and spend some time afterwards with your reading, your prayers, your silence. Don't receive the Eucharist unless you really believe it is the Body of Christ and unless you go to Confession. The Catholic Church that follows Pope John Paul 2, is the Church Jesus

established when he was on the earth. I know that if you don't have an authority, you have everyone deciding what they want to do or what they feel is right. I know that the Church goes back to the time of Jesus and is responsible for the Bible. Most important, I know Jesus is my Lord and Savior, He is real, and He is present in the Eucharist. Let us know if you are getting married and we will decide if we can come to the ceremony. I don't know what else to say about it. It's a very hard decision, not only financially, but otherwise.

After the wedding, we returned to Texas, and things in our lives were going great. We had built a strong network of like-minded people. We even offered to host the first "New Walk" Bible study for new Christians at our house. Everything seemed to be on the right track. But even with things going so well, I wanted to make sure I wasn't just following pure emotion again. I'd sincerely believed in Equinox, the MLM company that originally brought me to Texas, and I'd been wrong. It felt a little like getting out of a bad relationship and hesitating to jump into a new one, even if it feels amazing at the start.

A man named Walter Nusbaum, who worked at Denton Bible, gave me several books that provided evidence supporting the belief that Jesus Christ was a real historical figure, that He was crucified and rose from the dead. This was a big deal for me. After all, I used to believe in Santa Claus, the Easter Bunny, and the tooth fairy—so what if Jesus was just another story we were all told? The books that made the most impact on me were by Josh McDowell: *Evidence That Demands a Verdict* and *The New Evidence That Demands a Verdict 2*. Today, I'd recommend *The Case for Jesus* by Dr. Brant Pitre.

I was excited to find that there was actual evidence supporting the idea that Jesus wasn't just a made-up, feel-good story. The people influencing us at the time seemed genuine and truly cared about the best interests of both Pk and me. After living in so much darkness and sin for so many years, the pursuit of virtue—surrounded by well-meaning, sincere people—was incredibly attractive to me.

At one point, Pk mentioned to Walter that I'd been raised Catholic. Walter, a well-meaning and sincere non-Catholic Christian, made it his mission to ensure that Pk and I were "saved" and that I understood the so-called "flaws" in Catholic teachings. The truth was, I had no idea there was such a divide between Protestants and Catholics. Growing up, we never really talked about differences in Christian beliefs.

Walter opened his Bible and asked, "Tim, what do you think is necessary for someone to go to Heaven?"

I gave what I thought was the right answer: "You need to be a good person."

Walter then flipped to Romans 3:28 and asked me to read it aloud. The verse said, "For we maintain that a person is justified by faith apart from the works of the law."

"What does that say to you, Tim?" he asked.

Walter went on to explain that according to the Bible, we are justified and can go to Heaven without needing to perform good works. He said that we are "saved" by faith alone in Jesus Christ. He explained that all we needed to do was sincerely confess that Jesus is our Lord, believe He was crucified and rose from the dead for our sins, and we would be saved.

As a guy who was more into sports and parties than studying the Bible, this was all new to me. But even though it was foreign, something inside me told me there had to be more to the story. I told Walter I would look into it further.

# Chapter 7

# Searching for the Truth

I'm someone who is always seeking the truth—the facts. This became even more important to me after my experience with Equinox, where I was manipulated by emotions rather than facts. So, when it came to understanding the differences in Christian beliefs, I needed to get to the bottom of it. What were the facts? What were the differences between Catholic and non-Catholic doctrines? Which were rooted in history? Which were built on truth? And, most importantly, did it even matter which Christian denomination I followed as long as I believed in Jesus Christ as my savior?

We were deeply embedded in this new church and its culture, which was excellent at making people feel connected. It felt like we had discovered a whole new world. We only listened to Christian music, watched Christian movies, played on Fellowship Church's adult sports teams, volunteered in any way we could, and were part of small groups and Bible studies regularly. All our friends were from the church, and we were happy to be a part of this new culture and world we had never known existed.

Around this time, my mom sent me a VHS tape she had recorded, featuring several episodes of The Journey Home on EWTN, a Catholic television network.

The people being interviewed were highly educated non-Catholic Christians who had once believed that the Catholic Church taught things contrary to the Bible. This show has aired for over 25 years and airs every Monday night. Each episode tells the conversion story of someone coming from a non-Catholic or non-religious background into the Catholic Church.

I was impressed by the number of well-educated, non-Catholics who had studied their way into the Catholic Church. To this day, I've never heard of a Catholic leaving the Church because they studied their way out. *The Journey Home* claims that over 1,200 Protestant pastors have converted to Catholicism in the last 25 years.

Given that Pk and I had fully immersed ourselves in a non-Catholic environment, this presented a few challenges. First, how was I supposed to figure out who was right and who was wrong? And second, if I did discover that Catholicism was the truest representation of what Jesus taught, what were we supposed to do? Would we have to disconnect from all the new friends we'd made and come to love?

Watching those conversion stories was impressive, but I knew there were always two sides to every story. You might wonder, "Why does it matter? Why not just stick with what works for you and your wife?" The answer is simple: I didn't want to follow something that wasn't objectively true.

If Jesus Christ was truly the path to salvation and the way out of the darkness I had lived in for so long, then I wanted to follow what He taught. I wasn't interested in anyone's personal opinions about His teachings. I'm an all-or-nothing kind of guy. If we were going to do this "Christian" thing, I wanted to make sure we were doing it right and understanding exactly what Jesus wanted from us.

I've never been afraid to ask tough questions, so I set up a meeting with Fr. Mitch Pacwa and two leaders from

Denton Bible Church—Walter and John. I also invited Tim Staples, who is now a senior apologist at Catholic Answers, to my house to debate Walter and John on another occasion.

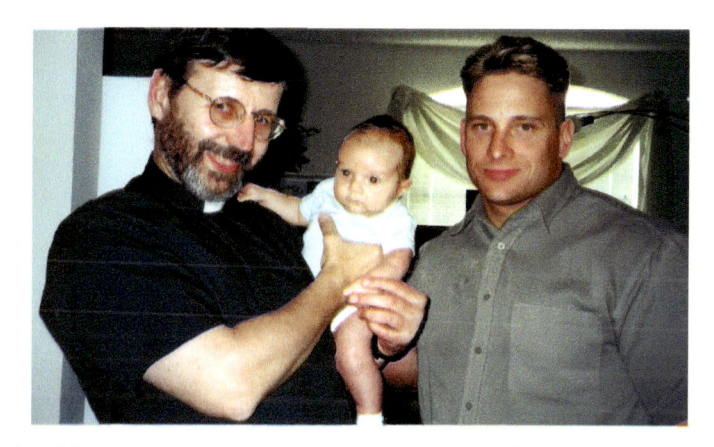

Father Mitch Pacwa holding my son Christian. Father Pacwa was at my house to discuss the differences with the leaders of Denton Bible church at my request.

The *Journey Home* program (www.ewtn.com) that aired every Monday night allows people to call/email questions. On August 6th, 1999, they read the following question followed by addressing me personally on behalf of my mother's request:

> Dear Marcus & David:
> I Am not sure how to characterize my question. I appreciate your time with all my questions. My son is studying the Church and I really don't like him relying on me for all his answers. He asked why we need Theologians? Doesn't Jesus want things to be simple? I answered that things have changed since the time of Jesus, and we need people who study and have the authority to find answers to questions that come up. Is there more that I could have said?
> Thanks
> —Pat Francis

I had been asking my mother every question under the sun as it relates to the Non-Catholic & Catholic Christian divide. My mother was not steeped in Catholic theology. She simply lived her faith like a saint.

I also started listening to every debate I could get my hands on between Catholics and Non-Catholic Christians.

I became obsessed with understanding the truth, and this caused some friction between Pk and me. She didn't have any issues with the theological debates, but she didn't like the emotional strain it was causing on our relationships, especially with the Bible study group we'd grown close to. I was transparent about everything I was learning and tried to share it with my buddy Rob and the men's group at Fellowship Church.

I remember my mother sending me a tape series called "Romanism in Romans" by a former Protestant pastor who converted to Catholicism by the name of Scott Hahn. Scott was asked to be the Dean of a Protestant seminary in his mid-20s and turned it down to become a lay Catholic. I literally typed every word that Scott said and brought it to my bible study group. We just happened to be reading through the book of Romans and discussing it in our Bible study. I was so naïve that I thought this would be a welcome discovery by the others.

Let me back up and explain something briefly. Martin Luther was a Catholic priest who became the founder of the Protestant (Protesting Catholics) faith. Martin Luther argued that justification is the doctrine on which the Church stands or falls. Remember the scripture verse that Walter had me read: Romans 3:28. "For we maintain that a person is justified by faith apart from the works of the law."

This was the very same verse in which Martin Luther inserted the word "alone" right after the word faith. He started the Protestant Church with two foundational principles that separated it from the Catholic Faith. These pillars were called "Faith Alone" and "Bible Alone." In my own words, Martin Luther believed that we are justified before God by "Faith Alone," not by any good works that we do. However, he did believe that if we didn't have good works, then ours was not a saving faith. He felt that Romans 3:28 said that we are justified by faith alone and not by any works.

Now, why is this important? Simply put, if Jesus Christ is real and our path to salvation, then understanding what is required to "be saved" is critical. Scott Hahn had previously taught the Book of Romans from Martin Luther's perspective many times. He went to a seminary to learn this perspective. However, he was now explaining verse by verse in the book of Romans how Martin Luther misunderstood the scripture in this book. I outlined this tape series word for word and brought it to the men's group.

Back to my men's group…the veterans/leaders were not very happy with me. One of them quoted a verse from 2 Timothy 2:23-24: "Don't have anything to do with foolish and stupid arguments because you know they produce quarrels. And the Lord's servant must not be quarrelsome but must be kind to everyone."

I was being accused of producing quarrels by bringing foolish and stupid arguments to the Bible Study. I was called out big time! Previously in my life, as you've learned, if someone were to call me out like that, I would have probably punched him in the mouth. I am not proud of that, but when confronted, fighting was a normal part of my past. I was shocked! I thought we were attempting to understand the book of Romans. Why wouldn't everyone be interested in a proper interpretation of this book if it was so important to our salvation?

Growing up in New Carlisle, Ohio, I had never heard the term "getting saved." But now that I was in Texas and attending a non-denominational mega-church, that's all they talked about. At the end of every service, they promoted three things:

1. Donating a minimum of 10% of your income.
2. Inviting others to attend the next service.
3. Saying the "sinner's prayer" to guarantee your ticket to heaven.

I became frustrated by the lack of desire for deeper study among my fellow Bible study members. They weren't interested in going beyond their personal interpretations and feelings about each Bible verse. But I wanted more than feelings. I wanted facts. Why wouldn't they want to investigate why there were so many denominations, all claiming to have the correct interpretation of the Bible?

I had no interest in simply attending weekly Bible studies to discuss how a two-thousand-year-old book made us "feel." One of my favorite quotes now is: "Facts don't care about your feelings." I needed to dig deeper and understand where these modern Christian teachings were coming from. Who had the authority to interpret the Bible?

It soon became clear to me that each denomination relied on its own source of authority for interpreting God's Word. If I had learned my theology from a Baptist school, I'd naturally believe in Baptist teachings. What I needed to discover was which interpretation aligned with ancient Christianityn and whose was a "Johnny Come Lately" version.

Around this time, I was attending a service at Fellowship Church with Pk when Pastor Ed Young said, "Jesus said this represents my body." I almost jumped out of my seat. I had studied enough by that point to know that Jesus said, "This is my body," not "this represents my body." My wife, knowing me well, squeezed my arm, signaling for me not to speak up right then.

It would've been one thing if the pastor had said, "Yes, Jesus said, 'This is my body,' but what He meant was 'This represents my body.'" But that's not what he said. My wife knows me too well. I'm not one to sit quietly when I think someone is distorting the truth. She saw my reaction and grabbed my arm, shaking her head as if to say, "Not now, please."

I set up an appointment to meet with Ed Young. Before our meeting, I gave him two things: a VCR tape of Dr. Kenneth Howell, a former Presbyterian minister who converted to Catholicism because of what he discovered in the Scriptures about the Eucharist. I also handed over a printout that outlined how all the early Church leaders from the first four centuries after Jesus' Resurrection interpreted His words when He said things like:

- "If anyone eats this bread, he will live forever."
- "Unless you eat the flesh of the Son of Man and drink His blood, you have no life in you."
- "He who eats My flesh and drinks My blood abides in Me."
- "He who eats Me will live because of Me."
- "He who eats this bread [His flesh] will live forever."
- "This is My body, this is My blood. If you eat My flesh and drink My blood, you will have eternal life."

Here's a sampling of what I gave to Ed Young:

**110 A.D.**
"They abstain from the Eucharist and from prayer because they do not confess that the Eucharist is the flesh of our Savior Jesus Christ, flesh which suffered for our sins and which the Father, in His goodness, raised up again."

**151 A.D.**
"The food which has been made into the Eucharist by the Eucharistic prayer set down by Him, and by the change of which our blood and flesh is nurtured, is both the flesh and the blood of that incarnated Jesus."

**189 A.D.**
"When, therefore, the mixed cup [wine and water] and the baked bread receive the Word of God and become the Eucharist, the body of Christ, and from these the substance of our flesh is increased and supported."

**350 A.D.**
"The bread and the wine of the Eucharist before the holy invocation of the adorable Trinity were simple bread and wine, but the invocation having been made, the bread becomes the body of Christ and the wine the blood of Christ."

"Do not, therefore, regard the bread and wine as simply that; for they are, according to the Master's declaration, the body and blood of Christ. Even though the senses suggest to you the other, let faith make you firm."

When I arrived for the meeting, I wasn't greeted by Ed but instead by his assistant, whose name, if I remember correctly, was Tracy. Tracy asked me what my issue was, and I told him. I explained that I couldn't find any Christians in the first 1,500 years of Christianity who had interpreted Jesus' words about eating His flesh and drinking His blood as just symbolic, as it was being taught at Fellowship Church. The same was true regarding the concept of getting "saved" once and being good to go. The same went for not baptizing infants and using "Bible alone" to guide us in our Christian walk. I could have gone on, but you get the picture. I gave them all the evidence to support my findings.

Tracy's response? "Well, Tim, we just don't see it that way."

That's it? That was the explanation for why they were teaching thousands of people every week something that completely contradicted how all early Christians had understood Jesus' teachings for 1,500 years?

Apparently, yes.

It's become clear to me that people who build huge empires or businesses are often more concerned with not losing what they've built than with seeking objective truth. It's human nature. As mentioned earlier, *"The Journey Home"* has reported that over 1,200 Protestant pastors have left their positions to become Catholic laypeople after researching the early Church. The famous convert to Catholicism, John Henry Cardinal Newman, once said, "To be deep in history is to cease to be Protestant."

I learned the Catholic faith by studying and listening to debates. I love hearing all sides of an argument. I'm like this with politics, too. Eventually, I became convinced that the Catholic Church is the most biblical and historically accurate representation of what Jesus Christ taught and what the Holy Spirit revealed to His disciples after He ascended into heaven. But here's where it became difficult: both my wife and the new network of friends we had made didn't want to hear anything about the Catholic faith. I gave everyone conversion tapes, books, and VCR tapes. No one cared. My wife wanted me to bite my tongue and just get along. She often said, "Catholics and Non-Catholics are basically teaching the same thing, just saying it differently."

That philosophy drove me nuts.

Over the years, I've given parish missions at Catholic churches across the country, and I've found that many "cradle Catholics" — people who've been Catholic from birth — are unaware of the historical truth behind what we believe and why. They're not only shocked by what they've never been taught, but they're also frustrated that they never learned it in the first place.

There's been a ton of literature written on these subjects, so I don't intend to write fifty pages on the theological differences between Catholic and non-Catholic Christians. However, if you're interested in what the Catholic Church teaches and why, I suggest three things:

> First, read the summary found on this site: [www.catholic.com/tract/pillar-of-fire-pillar-of-truth].
>
> Next, if you have a question about any topic (Mary, Purgatory, Salvation, Mass, Baptism, etc.), just Google that topic followed by "Catholic Answers." For example, if I wanted to know why Catholics "worship" Mary, I'd type "Mary Catholic Answers."
>
> Finally, you can go directly to www.Catholic.com and type your question in the search bar. In the meantime, here's a quick summary of some important differences I encountered. There are certainly more than just these, and I'm only speaking from my experience with non-denominational churches.

### Faith Alone vs. Faith + Works

## NON-CATHOLICS:

Good deeds have nothing to do with getting us to heaven. You say the sinner's prayer and really believe that Jesus died for you, and that guarantees your spot in heaven. They encourage living by the Bible and doing good, but they don't see good deeds as being connected to "being saved."

## CATHOLICS:

God gives us the grace to have both faith and to do good works. Our faith enables us to perform good works that are pleasing to God. Faith is not passive; it's alive, and it grows through our actions. These two verses from James explain it perfectly:

> James 2:21-22:
> "Was not Abraham our father justified by works, when he offered his son Isaac upon the altar? You see that faith was active along with his works, and faith was completed by works."

> James 2:24:
> "You see that a man is justified by works and NOT by faith alone." (This is actually the ONLY place in the Bible where the words "faith" and "alone" appear together — and it says NOT by faith alone.)

### Can Someone Lose His or Her Salvation?

## NON-CATHOLICS:

If you truly believe that Jesus is the Son of God and you give your life to Him in a moment of faith, there's nothing you can do to lose your salvation. However, some will say that if you return to a life of sin, then you were never really saved in the first place.

## CATHOLICS:

Early Christian thinkers put it simply:

Irenaeus (AD 180):

"Those who do not obey Him, being disinherited by Him, have ceased to be His sons."

Clement of Alexandria (AD 195):

"It is neither the faith, nor the love, nor the hope, nor the endurance of one day; rather, 'he who endures to the end will be saved.'"

## The Approved Guide for Your Faith

## NON-CATHOLICS:

The Bible is the only infallible guide God gave us to follow in the footsteps of Jesus. If it's not explicitly in the Bible, it's not essential for your salvation.

## CATHOLICS:

1. The Word of God = Written + Oral Tradition. Everything Jesus did and said were the words and actions of God. In John 21:25, it says, "Jesus did many other things as well. If every one of them were written down, I suppose that even the whole world would not have room for the books that would be written."

John Chrysostom said it best:

> "[Paul commands,] 'Therefore, brethren, stand fast and hold the traditions which you have been taught,

whether by word or by our letter' (2 Thess. 2:15). From this, it's clear that they didn't hand down everything by letter; much of it wasn't written."

2. Jesus never told us that only the Bible should be our guide for all Christian truth. The Bible says, "The Church is the Pillar and Foundation of Truth" (1 Timothy 3:15). John, one of Jesus' disciples, taught a man named Polycarp, who later taught Irenaeus. Irenaeus said this:

"Since therefore we have such proofs, it is not necessary to seek the truth among others, which it is easy to obtain from the Church; since the apostles, like a rich man [depositing his money] in a bank, lodged in her hands most copiously all things pertaining to the truth, so that every man, whosoever will, can draw from her the water of life."

The Catholic belief about authority is not based on the Bible alone. The Church is the "Pillar and Foundation of Truth," and the Word of God, both written and oral, was entrusted to the Church, just as we deposit money into a bank.

## In Summary

- The Bible never teaches that God's Word is confined to written text, or that everything Christians believe is explicitly in the Bible.
- The Bible teaches that God's Word also exists in oral form as Sacred Tradition.
- Non-Catholic Christians accept the oral tradition of the Church that decided which books would make up the Bible.

## The Sacraments

**NON-CATHOLICS:**

We should be baptized after we give our life to Christ by saying the sinner's prayer and meaning it sincerely. Once a month, we remember Jesus' sacrifice by sharing grape juice and crackers to symbolize the Last Supper. Marriage is between a man and a woman and can only be dissolved in cases of infidelity or abuse. Baptism itself doesn't save you; you are saved the moment you confess with your mouth and believe in your heart that Jesus is Lord. Baptism and the Lord's Supper are purely symbolic. There's no need to baptize infants since they haven't yet made the personal decision to follow Christ.

All our sins—past, present, and future—are forgiven when we become Christians. You don't need to confess to a priest; just go straight to God.

**CATHOLICS:**

To quote from [Catholic.com](http://www.catholic.com) (Pillar of Fire, Pillar of Truth):

> "Jesus promised that He would not leave us orphans (John 14:18), but would send the Holy Spirit to guide and protect us (John 15:26). He gave us the Sacraments to heal, feed, and strengthen us. The seven Sacraments—Baptism, the Eucharist, Penance (also called Reconciliation or Confession), Confirmation, Holy Orders, Matrimony, and the Anointing of the Sick—are not just symbols. They are signs that convey God's grace and love."

### Baptism

Baptism is essential for cleansing our souls of both original and personal sin. Even infants need this cleansing from original sin, which is why the early Christians always practiced infant baptism. St. Origen captured this beautifully when he said, "The Church received from the apostles the tradition of giving baptism even to infants. The apostles, to whom were committed the secrets of the divine Sacraments, knew there are in everyone innate stains of [original] sin, which must be washed away through water and the Spirit."

St. Augustine echoed this when he said, "The custom of Mother Church in baptizing infants is certainly not to be scorned . . . nor is it to be believed that its tradition is anything except apostolic."

Under the Old Covenant, people had their children circumcised as a sign of the covenant—a binding oath between them and God. Baptism now replaces circumcision in the New Covenant, and this New Covenant is far more powerful than the Old. (See Heb. 10:1; Col. 2:17; Heb. 8:6.)

The only debate in the early Church was whether to wait eight days to baptize a newborn. Eventually, it was decided that baptism should happen right away. It was never a question of whether babies should be baptized. As Cyprian of Carthage (A.D. 253) put it:

> "As to what pertains to the case of infants: You [Fidus] said that they ought not to be baptized within the second or third day after their birth, that the old law of circumcision must be taken into consideration, and that you did not think that one should be baptized and sanctified within the eighth day after his birth. In our council it seemed to us far otherwise. No one agreed to the course which you thought should be taken. Rather, we all judge that the mercy and grace of God ought to be denied to no man born."

Dr. David Anders, in his article "How John Calvin Made Me Catholic" on www.calledtocommunion.com, quoted John Calvin—one of the key figures in Protestant history—saying:

> "He never taught the Evangelical doctrine that one is 'born again' through personal conversion. Instead, he associated regeneration with baptism and taught that to neglect baptism was to refuse salvation. He also allowed no diversity over the manner of its reception. Anabaptists in Geneva (those who practiced adult baptism) were jailed and forced to repent. Calvin taught that Anabaptists, by refusing the sacrament to their children, had placed themselves outside the faith."

It's ironic because the leaders at Denton Bible, who were mentoring Pk and me, were big John Calvin supporters. They would say their view of salvation was "Calvinist." But according to Calvin, their understanding of baptism "placed themselves outside the faith." I remember being at Walter's house when he tried to convince me that when the apostle Peter said, "Baptism now saves you" (1 Pet. 3:21), he wasn't talking about water baptism actually saving you. Here was a well-meaning, Bible-educated man who called himself a "Calvinist" but was interpreting scripture in a way that, according to Calvin, put him "outside the faith." This showed me that using the "Bible only" approach couldn't possibly work.

## Confession to a Priest

Jesus told Peter, "You are rock, and upon this rock, I will build my Church." He also said, "Whatever you bind on earth will be bound in Heaven, and whatever you loose on earth will be loosed in Heaven." Later, Jesus said to His apostles, "Receive the Holy Spirit. If you forgive the sins of any, they are forgiven; if you retain the sins of any, they are retained."

Confession is a gift from God that allows priests to forgive or retain sins on behalf of Jesus Christ.

John Chrysostom put it powerfully: "Priests have received a power which God has given neither to angels nor to archangels. It was said to them: 'Whatsoever you shall bind on earth shall be bound in heaven; and whatsoever you shall loose shall be loosed.' Temporal rulers have indeed the power of binding; but they can only bind the body. Priests, in contrast, can bind with a bond which pertains to the soul itself and transcends the very heavens. Did [God] not give them all the powers of heaven? 'Whose sins you shall forgive,' He says, 'they are forgiven them; whose sins you shall retain, they are retained.' What greater power is there than this? The Father has given all judgment to the Son. And now I see the Son placing all this power in the hands of men." (Matt. 10:40; John 20:21–23.)

The grace we receive from confession strengthens us to avoid future sin.

### The Lord's Supper, Communion, Mass

To quote from Catholic.com once again, "The sacrifice of Christ on the cross occurred 'once for all' and it cannot be repeated (Heb. 9:28). Christ does not 'die again' during Mass, but the very same sacrifice that occurred on Calvary is made present on the altar. This is why the Mass is not 'another' sacrifice but rather a participation in the same, once-for-all sacrifice of Christ on the cross."

Paul reminds us that the bread and wine truly become, through a miracle of God's grace, the actual body and blood of Jesus: "Anyone who eats and drinks without recognizing the body of the Lord eats and drinks judgment on himself" (1 Cor. 11:27–29).

After the consecration of the bread and wine, no bread or wine remains on the altar. Only Jesus Himself, under the appearance of bread and wine, remains. As I mentioned earlier, all the early Christians believed this.

The bottom line is that everything I read, watched, and listened to provided overwhelming evidence that many of the teachings in modern American mega-churches contradicted what the ancient Christians, known as the Church Fathers, taught. Why would anyone spend their time listening to people teach the Christian faith if they knew it was contrary to what Jesus taught and passed on to His disciples?

To be clear, I'm not saying that these mega-church pastors and leaders are intentionally misleading people. It's just that the longer you believe something to be true, the harder it is to change your viewpoint. We all tend to see the world through the lens that has shaped our understanding. This is true for everything we've been taught and everything we've bought into.

I was excited about what I had learned—finally, the truth! I had done the work, studied, and grown, but the question was, what now? My wife wanted me to "stay the course" and not disrupt the new relationships we had built. But I wanted to follow the truth, which was leading me back to the Catholic faith with a new appreciation for the miracle of the Mass.

## Christian Michael Francis Joins the Family

On February 15, 2001, after 16 hours of labor and an emergency C-section, our first child was born: Christian Michael Francis. Although I was still searching and unsure about many things, one thing I knew for certain was that I did not want to miss out on any important moments in my son's life. At the time, I wasn't sure what vehicle would provide that for us, but now, at 23 years old, Christian has shown me that God provided more than I could have imagined back then.

What I'm most proud of is Christian's commitment to his Catholic faith. He has taken ownership of his faith journey and knows exactly why he believes what he believes.

**Christian, Pk, and me through the years.**

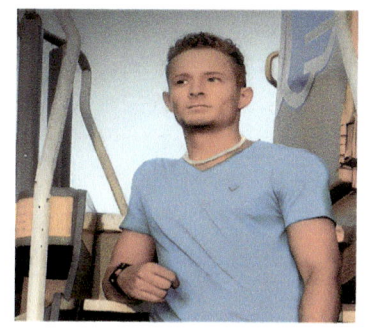

# Chapter 8

# Signs From God – Science Tests Faith

Mom handed me a VCR tape where she had recorded part of a two-hour television special called *Signs from God—Science Tests Faith*. This special first aired on the Fox Network in July 1999. Now, if you're interested, you can watch the full video online at [www.ScienceTestsFaith.com].

The special featured Mike Willesee, A famous TV star, a well-known investigative journalist from Australia, and a household name at the time. Mike didn't believe in God or anything supernatural. But his lawyer challenged him to investigate a woman supposedly experiencing the "stigmata"—something I had never heard of before.

"Stigmata" refers to a supernatural phenomenon where certain followers of Christ bear the physical wounds that Jesus suffered during His Passion—wounds on their hands, feet, side, face, and head. It's considered an extraordinary and rare gift. The people who bear these wounds are called "Victim Souls," and the belief is that their suffering is united with Christ's suffering, offering redemption for others.

Here are a few Bible verses that support this teaching:

> Colossians 1:24: "In my flesh, I complete what is lacking in Christ's afflictions for the sake of the body, that is, the Church."

> Romans 8:16-17: "It is the Spirit himself bearing witness with our spirit that we are children of God, and if children, then heirs, heirs of God and fellow heirs with Christ, provided we suffer with Him in order that we may also be glorified with Him."
>
> 1 Peter 18:21: "For to this you have been called, because Christ also suffered for you, leaving you an example, that you should follow in His steps."
>
> Philippians 1:29: "For it has been granted to you that for the sake of Christ you should not only believe in Him but also suffer for His sake."
>
> Luke 9:23: "If anyone wishes to come after Me, he must deny himself and take up his cross daily and follow Me."

The attorney who challenged Mike Willesee was a man named Ron Tesoriero, and the woman in question was Catalina (Katya) Rivas. Catalina was a grandmother with only a seventh-grade education, but she claimed to receive messages directly from Jesus. Ron, in his book *My Human Heart*, writes about how Catalina predicted her own stigmata:

> "On Good Friday, 1999, there was an unprecedented prediction of a supernatural event. Before three cameras and five witnesses besides myself, Katya said, 'Jesus said I will have the stigmata on the day after the feast of Corpus Christi. It may be filmed for all to see.'" (Pg. 79)

The network hired Mike Willesee to fly to Bolivia with a film crew and capture the event. But when they arrived, Catalina said that Jesus had communicated that the timing wasn't right: "Jesus says it is not the right time. Tell Mike and Ron that there will be no stigmata tomorrow. He says it will be in His time, and you must learn to trust Him" (Pg. 74).

Disappointed but undeterred, the crew stayed in Bolivia. The following day, Catalina received another message: "It will happen on the day after Corpus Christi, and you will be able to come with witnesses and film what happens. I will have wounds that signify the Passion of Christ on my head, my feet, and my hands. It will start around noon and end just after 3 PM, and it will heal by the next day. I know this will happen because Jesus said it will, and I believe Him, and I trust Him" (Pg. 74).

Mike had spent his career interviewing prime ministers, movie stars, criminals, and sports legends. But just two months before he passed away from throat cancer in 2017, Ron interviewed him again, and Mike said, "Of all the stories I've covered, this one was the most important of my life. Everything else pales in comparison."

Alastair Thompson, a journalist from New Zealand, watched the special and remarked, "Put it this way—this is either the biggest hoax of the 20th Century, in which case it would have to be a fairly huge conspiracy, or the most important moment of the century, if not the whole millennium."

I remember sitting in my house in Euless, Texas, watching this unfold on my big screen TV. At the time, I had no idea that the stigmata was linked to the Catholic faith. I was simply mesmerized by the possibility that this might be supernatural evidence for believing in Jesus Christ. Up to that point, I had heard historical arguments for why Jesus was real and rose from the dead. But here I was, watching what seemed like a modern-day manifestation that Jesus was still active in the world today.

# From the Crack House to God's House

As Predicted, on June 4, the wounds of Christ's crucifixion began to appear on Katya's body and were professionally filmed with embedded timecodes.

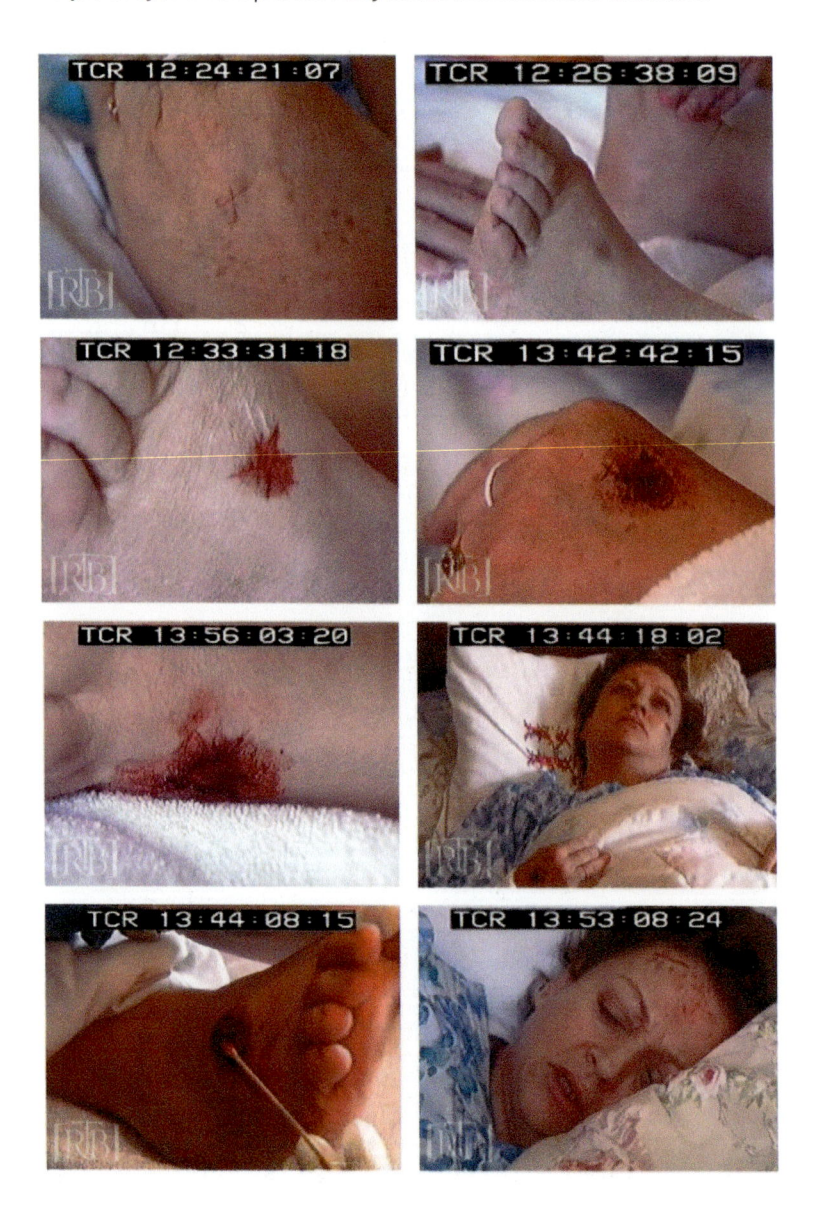

I had three burning questions:

1. Is this real? Did it actually happen?

2. If it is real, how do we know it's from God and not an evil spirit deceiving people?

3. If it's real and it's from God, what's the message behind it? What's the takeaway?

I called the Fox TV station and tried to find the rest of the show, but when I called the Fox station, they didn't have any way for me to access it. I even reached out to the priest who had appeared in the show, but he was brief and dismissive. There was no book, no website, no follow-up anywhere. I kept sharing the tape with friends, and every time, they had the same reaction: "Wow! Is this real? But what does it all mean?"

It took me ten years to answer those questions. I'll get into that later.

Pk didn't want to become Catholic, and I couldn't ignore all the evidence I had gathered about the early Christian Church—the faith of the apostles and how they lived for the first 1500 years after Christ's resurrection.

Slowly, a divide started growing between us. Moving from the bar scene to the Bible scene had already been a big change, and now I was leaning toward Catholicism while feeling increasingly isolated. The demonic world preys on division—whether in families, countries, or the world. And we were feeling it.

Fr. Vincent Lampert, the Exorcist for the Diocese of Indianapolis, teaches that demons thrive when they can isolate us from the support we receive from community. One of his teachers had taught him that the devil uses a four-stage plan of attack on us. It begins with deception, which leads to division, which leads to diversion, and ends in discouragement. I will go into more depth on this later in the book This pattern was playing out in my life then—and even now, I can still see it.

Isolated from my wife and my new community, I reached back to my old one. The devil, as always, uses "the world and the flesh" to lead us to destruction when we're at our weakest. And all it takes for the demonic to gain a foothold is an invitation.

Fr. Vincent warns: "Habitual sin in the form of alcohol and drug abuse can be an entry point for evil."

Looking back, I can see how the perfect storm was brewing in my life. Fr. Vincent also identified eight major ways people open the door to evil. Two of those were my gateways: (1) Habitual sin through alcohol and drug abuse, and (2) Unhealed broken relationships. Fr. Vincent put it this way: "When we experience animosity, bitterness, resentment, anger, and revenge, we allow evil to keep its grip on us..."

## A Step Backward

Bitterness and resentment, along with alcohol, were a direct path to further division between Pk and me. One night, we were in Dallas celebrating New Year's Eve with some friends. Pk's friend Melissa brought along a guy from New York. He didn't know anything about my past with alcohol and drugs. Before I knew it, he and I were at the bar, drinking. It didn't take much—just a beer and a few shots—and suddenly, something switched in my brain. That old familiar craving kicked in, and I was on the hunt for the next high. Without saying a word, I left the bar. I didn't even think twice about leaving my credit card behind since I had opened a tab. I hopped in a cab and headed straight for the rough part of town, where I quickly found someone to sell me crack.

I know it sounds insane now, but when that trigger gets pulled, you become like a dog chasing its bone. The next morning, when I woke up in the hotel room, I wished it had all been a bad dream—but it wasn't.

When my brain locks onto that high, it's like tunnel vision. All logic goes out the window. The Yale Medicine website states: "When a person develops an addiction to a substance, it's because the brain has started to change. Addictive substances trigger an outsized response when they hit the brain. Instead of a simple, pleasurable surge of dopamine, drugs like opioids, cocaine, or nicotine cause dopamine to flood the reward pathway—ten times more than a natural reward. The brain remembers this surge and associates it with the addictive substance."

I know this all too well. While I don't want to excuse my behavior, the facts are the facts.

When you're chasing a drug, it's like you're a man on a mission. St. Paul said it best in Galatians 5:17: "For the desires of the flesh are against the Spirit, and the desires of the Spirit are against the flesh; for these are opposed to each other, to keep you from doing the things you want to do."

He goes even deeper in Romans 7:16, 19, and 23: "I do not understand my own actions. For I do not do what I want, but I do the very thing I hate... For I do not the good that I want, but the evil I do not want is what I do... I see in my members another law at war with the law of my mind and making me captive to the law of sin that dwells in my members."

My life went from bad to worse in the blink of an eye. The disappointment, disgust, and discouragement were overwhelming. Here I was trying to share the ancient Christian path with others, and before I knew it, I was back in the Devil's hands, using what I now call "The Devil Stick." Evil spirits thrive on hypocrisy, and I had given them an open door.

There's a verse in the Bible that says, "If a house is divided against itself, that house will not be able to stand" (Mark 3:25). My house was already divided, and now I had shattered it into a million pieces. It would take a miracle to put it back together.

I am eternally grateful for the strong, committed Christian women who surrounded Pk and encouraged her to fight for our marriage. They told her to "stand by her man."

We took two paths to wage the war against the world, the flesh, and the devil. First, we started seeing Richard, a calm and thoughtful Christian marriage counselor. He was devoted to helping us. Second, I joined a Narcotics Anonymous (NA) group.

After listening to our stories, Richard hit the nail on the head. He said, "My vision is that you, Tim, are a lion in a cage, and Pk is the zookeeper."

He was spot on. As much as I loved the pursuit of virtue and character, I felt isolated and stripped of what I used to consider "normal social fun." It took me years to learn how to enjoy a party atmosphere without resorting to cocaine to take things to the next level.

As I mentioned earlier, I'm an extrovert by nature, always full of energy, and I love meeting and talking with people. I used to see that as one of my strengths. But our counselor helped me realize something important—overusing a strength can turn it into a weakness.

Here's what I mean...

Let's say you're a great speaker, a natural entertainer. Overuse that strength, and you might become a terrible listener. Or if your strength is keeping a neat and organized home, you might unintentionally make guests feel uncomfortable, as if you're cleaning up before they're even finished eating.

For me, my impulsivity and naivety were my

weaknesses. I would jump into things without thinking them through. That was a hard pill to swallow, but it was one I needed to face if I was going to change.

McLean Hospital describes it perfectly: "Addiction swaps the everyday desires of the brain with those of the drug you're addicted to. You no longer enjoy what other people do as the brain changes." That was me to a T. It took years to enjoy the simple things again.

Richard's counseling, along with NA meetings, were helpful. But I needed something beyond the natural—I needed something supernatural to win this war.

Letter from Mom — Early 2000:

> Dad and I had a talk about Christian Michael's baptism. We both feel strongly that we should share our thoughts with you. We're not telling you what to do—we just want to give you our opinion. We both really want him to be baptized, and we hope that you and Pk can come to a decision about what direction you're going to take.

Letter from Mom — December 2, 2001:

> You've been on my mind since I got back home. I keep thinking about when you talked about how guilty you feel over things in your past. I mentioned Confession to you then, and I still think about that. You can't keep making decisions for your life based on guilt from the past—I really believe that's been a big part of what's holding you back.
>
> I want to ask you to do two things while you're still figuring out who you are and what direction to take. First, bless yourself every day with holy water. I do this every morning for all of you. I name each of

you and sprinkle holy water over myself. Second, pray at least one decade of the rosary each day, just like Scott Hahn does. You can pick your own intention, but be bold—pray for something that seems impossible or that's really weighing on your heart.

When I was on the plane, they gave instructions about what to do if the oxygen mask drops down. They said if you're with a child, you need to put your own mask on first before helping them. It really struck me that we have to take care of ourselves spiritually before we can truly help others. I've been thinking a lot about Confession for myself and others. I believe people go through life trying to fight their inner battles on their own, but we Catholics have the help we need—if we actually use it.

### Whose Sins You Forgive Are Forgiven

I had heard and read enough to convince me that I needed to go to Confession, for the first time in over fifteen years. The early Christian world used to call St. John Chrysostom "The Golden Mouth" because of his powerful sermons. He had something to say about the role of priests that really hit home for me, and it's worth sharing again:

> "Priests have received a power which God has given neither to angels nor to archangels. It was said to them: 'Whatsoever you shall bind on earth shall be bound in heaven; and whatsoever you shall loose, shall be loosed.' Temporal rulers have indeed the power of binding; but they can only bind the body. Priests, in contrast, can bind with a bond which pertains to the soul itself and transcends the very heavens. Did God not give them all the powers of

heaven? 'Whose sins you shall forgive,' he says, 'they are forgiven them; whose sins you shall retain, they are retained.' What greater power is there than this? The Father has given all judgment to the Son. And now I see the Son placing all this power in the hands of men" (Matt. 10:40; John 20:21–23).

I went to St. Michael's in Bedford, Texas. Isn't it something that my mom always encouraged me to lean on St. Michael, just like she did whenever she was worried about us? And now here I was, walking into St. Michael's for my first Confession in fifteen years. Oh, and by the way, we named our first-born son Christian "Michael"—I don't believe that's a coincidence at all.

Confession wasn't easy, and it definitely wasn't comfortable, but I can't tell you how I felt afterward—liberated, free, unburdened, with a sense of peace I hadn't experienced, maybe ever. That same feeling comes over me every time I've gone since. If I had heard someone say what I just did after my experience with Equinox, I probably would've thought it was all in their head—a placebo effect. But after diving into the biblical, historical, and supernatural evidence, I'm convinced that baptism and Confession are more than just rituals—they're real, supernatural forces that fight evil. I now understand what Peter meant when he said, "Baptism now saves you" (1 Pet. 3:21).

Christian and our second child, our daughter Hailey, were baptized on November 12th, 2004, at St. Michael's:

FROM THE CRACK HOUSE TO GOD'S HOUSE

Left to right: Cindy, Pk (with Hailey). Priest, Me (with Christian), Mike (my brother):

## The Compromise

Pk and I came to a compromise: we'd go to both the mega-Church service and Catholic Mass every weekend. Initially, I didn't want my kids learning the wrong version of Christian teachings (as I mentioned earlier in the book), but eventually, I realized hearing all sides of an argument can actually help ground you in what you believe. The sermons at Fellowship Church by Ed Young helped me live a more virtue-driven life. The only time I struggled was when Ed occasionally dived into theology.

The whole "you're saved once and for all" mentality never sat right with me. Let me give you an example. One of the guys in our Bible study was struggling with sleeping around, even though he wasn't married. He had been taught that once you "get saved," no matter what happens afterward, you're still saved. Sure, you might be backsliding, but your salvation was guaranteed. They also taught that if you were truly saved, you'd naturally want to please God and show the fruits of the Spirit.

Now, if Christianity is true, and there really is a heaven and a hell, imagine how terrible it would be for someone to believe they're saved based on faulty teachings. How can someone live in sin and still expect to go to heaven? The Bible—both in its written form and in oral tradition—teaches that we're in a constant battle between the flesh and the spirit, and only those who "persevere to the end" will be saved.

You can't have it both ways. Either the bread and wine truly become the body and blood of Christ, or they don't. Either confession to a priest is necessary, or it isn't. Either it's essential to baptize your children to cleanse them of original sin, or baptism is just an outward sign of a "born-again" experience that should happen once they're old enough to mean it.

These are fundamental differences that are impossible to ignore.

I remember reading *Will the Real Heretics Please Stand Up* by David Bercot. He's a non-Catholic Christian who researched the beliefs and practices of early Christians from A.D. 100-325. He was shocked to find out that what early Christians believed was completely different from what many modern non-Catholic Christians believe today. They didn't believe in "once saved, always saved." They didn't believe in salvation by "faith alone." This was yet another confirmation that what was being preached and taught in the non-denominational churches I was attending and listening to was not in line with what Jesus had passed on to His disciples.

# From the Crack House to God's House

Letter from Mom — November 17, 2002:

St. Jude has been my special prayer partner for you. When I don't know how to pray, I ask for his help, and finally, I've felt his help in praying for you. You have been given some special gifts, and I know the Lord wants you to use them. He'll guide you, but you have to get right with Him first. My prayers for you have been to ask the Lord that if you're meant to be successful, you first need to straighten out the rest of your life. Maybe the Lord is saying you have to be right with Him before He'll guide you in the rest. Start each day with prayer. Make it a priority. SEEK THE KINGDOM OF GOD FIRST in all you do.

## There Are Angels Among Us

Years ago, I was driving home from a late night out with some old "party friends." It was around 4 AM, and I must have fallen asleep at the wheel. The next thing I remember was waking up as my car flew through a grassy field. I had driven off the highway, crossed over a service road, and ended up in a deep ditch. My car had gone so far down the hill that the tow truck couldn't even reach it. It was raining, too. I had missed a telephone pole by just five feet and stopped about twenty yards from a bridge. I'd been going full speed when I veered off the road, landing on a small hill, some twenty yards away. Amazingly, I didn't have a single scratch on me!

Looking back, it seems almost impossible that I wasn't severely injured, or worse, killed. And when I think about what that Protestant pastor said—"What makes you think you can live like hell and still go to heaven?"—I know without a doubt that I was "living like hell" that night. But by the power of my mother's prayers, I believe my life and my soul were saved that night. I feel that with my whole heart.

# Signs From God – Science Tests Faith

Letter from Mom — January 6, 2003:

> Don't forget to start each day with prayer. If the Church is open, go spend some time in front of the Blessed Sacrament and give the Lord your problems and worries, asking Him for help. Try to go to daily Mass when you can. I can tell the difference in myself when I go regularly and when I don't. Don't forget St. Jude either—he's a special saint for you. I left you a prayer of his, but of course, you don't always have to say a certain prayer.

Letter from Mom — December 5, 2003:

> There was a time when my life was all mixed up, and I turned to the book of Job to find out what the Bible had to say about suffering. I've underlined a lot of things in the Bible that have spoken to me at different times. In the book of Job, I found only four places I underlined, and one of them really stood out to me. In Chapter 2, verse 10, Job had been struck with boils, and his wife told him that he should curse God and die. But he said to her, "Are you even going to speak like senseless women do? We accept good things from God, and should we not accept evil?"

God doesn't cause evil, but He allows it for a reason. We don't always understand the reason, but we have to trust Him.

The Last Letter from Mom — December 17, 2003:

> The picture on the front of the Christmas card I'm sending you is from a Shepherd's of Christ prayer

center. It all started in 1996 when the Blessed Mother's image appeared on the side of a bank building in Clearwater, Florida. When it first happened, it made the news, but you never hear about it now. She appeared on that bank building and told a visionary that people were too worried about money and the material things of the world. We need to follow Jesus.

The visionary who received that message about Mary appearing on the bank building shared many other messages that were compiled into a book called *The Blue Book*. My mom references The *Blue Book* in her journal. Her letter from December 17th ended with her sharing the Florida address where she and Dad would be staying after December 30th.

Dad had retired from Wright Patterson Air Force Base in 1992, and Mom became a secretary for Bethel Local Schools in 1988. For fifteen years, Dad had waited for Mom to retire so they could travel together. She finally retired in 2003, and Dad had rented a place for them to stay for three months in Sebring, Florida, starting in January 2004.

Mom's Prayer Journal — December 25, 2003:

> The *Blue Book* gives the message to wait upon your Lord and trust Him. Please, Lord, take care of the car, the furnace, the phone, my back, the cell phone, the packing. Please, Lord, take care of everything needed for our trip. Please stay close and bless us. I need Your wisdom. I need Your strength. Dear Blessed Mother, I need Your guidance in all things. I am fearful because I don't like change. Please bless Ed, Paul, and Phil in hunting. May they be successful and safe. I need to go to Church tomorrow. I can't go three days without receiving You, Lord.

# Chapter 9

# The Worst Day of My Life

On January 2, 2004, the phone rang. The caller ID showed it was my brother, Paul. I handed the phone to my three-year-old son, Christian, to say hello to his uncle. I heard Paul say in an urgent tone, "Christian, put your dad on the phone!"

I grabbed the phone, "What's up, Paul?"

"You need to get to Georgia right away. Mom had a massive heart attack while driving with Dad. They rushed her to the hospital. She's in a coma, and they don't think she'll make it through the night!"

I grabbed my wife and son, and we rushed to the airport. It felt like I had been kicked in the stomach. I could barely catch my breath.

My mom was at Spalding Medical Center in Griffin, Georgia. When I got to the hospital, it was gut-wrenching to see her in a coma and my dad, tears dripping down his face, in complete shock.

She died 17 days later, on January 19th. Those 17 days were the most painful of my life. My entire family was on an emotional roller coaster—not just day to day, but often minute to minute. One moment, we were given hope of her recovery, and the next, we were told there was no chance. I spoke at her funeral.

**Here's what I read:**

"Mom was taken to the emergency room in Georgia on January 2nd, on her way to Florida to spend three months of vacation with my dad after they both retired. As strange as this might sound, I had the great privilege of spending the next 17 days caring for my mom in hopes of her recovery. I say 'privilege,' not because of the heartbreaking circumstances, but because it gave me the chance to serve the woman who had spent 35 years serving me. As I sat by her bedside, rubbing her feet while she was in a coma, my brother made a joke about how Mom had never had so many foot massages in her 65 years. We laughed, but later, that gesture touched me in a very profound way. I cried, realizing the beautiful symbolism in what I was doing. All my life, my mom had served me with those hands and feet. What an honor it was to be there, feeding her, rubbing her feet, and comforting her. I only wish it could have been under different circumstances.

"The day after she passed, I was walking behind my dad's truck, and I noticed an old black snow boot in the bed of the truck. I stopped and just stared at it, my mind racing back to when I was an 8-year-old boy. It was one of the very same boots I had worn for sledding at Smith Park. And, of course, Dad still had it, because if you know him, you know he makes everything last forever. All I could think about was coming inside after sledding, and Mom making us sit down in the utility room before entering the kitchen, so she could pull off our boots. She would rub our feet and then cook us a warm meal. For 35 years, she slaved and served to make life more comfortable for me. All I wanted was more time to serve her in return, to make her life as comfortable as she had made mine.

"January 2nd–19th will always be etched deep in my heart. What a roller coaster ride. The pain, the love, the realizations that came because of Mom's heart condition—how fitting. Her loving heart kept our family bonded for 40 years, and now, that same heart, worn and damaged, brought us even closer. For those of you who knew Mom, you know that her only wish was for her family and friends to come to Christ through the Catholic Church. Nothing would have made her happier than seeing her husband and all of her kids praying together, receiving Christ in the Eucharist together, and hugging each other. That's exactly what happened from January 2nd to January 19th.

"For years, doctors had said that Mom's heart was twice the size of a normal heart. Medically speaking, she had an enlarged heart for many years. But if you knew Mom, you didn't need a doctor to tell you that. You could see the size of her heart in her actions, in her generosity, in the way she loved everyone she met. That's how you explain all the people sitting here today, so deeply impacted by someone as humble, gentle, and unassuming as Mom.

"After two weeks of praying, crying, feeding, and watching her fight for every breath, I stood there on January 19th, just past noon, and watched her slowly pass. There was nothing I could do except watch as the vitals faded and she took her last breath. I wanted her to live so badly, but not for her—for me. I wanted more time to serve my mom, the way she had served me.

"I believe there are two reasons she let go. First, she didn't want to burden my family with her recovery. That was her selfless nature. And second, God decided it was her time to rest in heaven. Her work on earth was done. I love you, Mom. Don't worry—you always did. We will take good care of each other here on earth until we meet you again in heaven."

After we buried Mom, I stayed with Dad for about a week. Watching my mom die and seeing her lowered into the ground was unimaginably hard, but one of the hardest things I had to do was leave my parents' house and fly back to Texas. There was nothing I could do to take away my dad's pain. As I flew out of Dayton back to Texas, tears streamed down my face.

# Chapter 10

# Moving Forward

**Hailey Through the Years**

Just a few months after my mom passed, my one and only baby girl was born—Hailey Alexandra Patricia Francis, on August 14, 2004. Hailey has always been Daddy's girl, no doubt about that. Over the years, I've been blessed to spend more time with her than she probably would have preferred! We've fished, camped, I coached her in basketball, and we've spent countless hours traveling across the United States together as a family. My wife and boys will tell you that Hailey always gets her way with Dad. She and I are alike in that sense—we both just want to have fun. If there were ever a song that could perfectly describe Hailey, it would be "Girls Just Want to Have Fun."

**Have another shot, just one more beer...**

Now we've arrived at the date that lives in infamy for me, which I mentioned earlier in this book. I'll repeat it here now that you have a better understanding of who I am, the battles I've faced—most of them created by my own choices. Maybe now, as you read this again, you'll see it more clearly, knowing that I'm a recovering drug addict who has spent decades fighting for my sanity and my family.

In 2005, I was living in Texas, married with kids, when I got an invitation to my friend Mike Bame's wedding in Ohio. This was about a year and a half after my mom had passed, and her death had shaken me to my core. I don't presume to say that I loved my mom more than anyone else loves theirs, but when she died, I felt utterly lost. It was like a void had opened up, a hole that no one and nothing could fill. She had been the glue of our family, and when she was gone, everything felt off-balance. So, the chance to see my family and reconnect with old college friends at the wedding felt like a lifeline. My brother Paul was also hosting a family get-together with all my siblings, their spouses, and their children, which made the trip even more important to me.

At that time, I felt the weight of being separated from

my family, living in another state, and missing out on so many birthdays, sporting events, and fishing trips with Dad. Being back home with them meant everything to me. But you wouldn't have known it by the way I acted after the wedding.

My college friends knew I liked to party, but none of them, except maybe my brother Mike, had any idea how far my cocaine and crack addiction had spiraled after college. Mike knew a little because I had confided in him back in 1997, and I'm sure he told Mom, but neither of them knew the full extent of my problem.

The wedding and reception were as fun as I'd hoped they would be. Everyone was having a great time. Afterward, some of my old college buddies wanted to head to one of our favorite clubs, a country bar called Club Dance in Reynoldsburg, Ohio. It was connected to a smaller bar called Bourbon Street, and we used to go there all the time during our college days.

You know how certain sights or smells can trigger a memory you haven't thought about in years? Well, that's what happened to me that night. The combination of being back at that old bar, already buzzed from the reception, and seeing familiar faces brought me right back to my partying days. I was in full relapse mode.

I'm reminded of the Kenny Chesney song, "I've Been There," where he sings, "The devil takes your hand and says no fear, have another shot, just one more beer." That's exactly what happened to me. I'm not making excuses, but I get it. That night, I crossed paths with someone who had access to cocaine, and it all went downhill from there.

My memory of the night is fuzzy, but I know I ended up in a car with people I didn't know, then at a stranger's house smoking crack. At some point, I was in an abandoned house with other addicts.

Thankfully, my brother Mike remembers more of that night than I do. This is how he tells it:

> "You disappeared from the Bame wedding and never showed up at Paul's the next day. We called your friends, but no one knew where you were. Somehow, we finally got a lead on where to find you. When we reached you, you told us where you were. Since we were in New Carlisle, I asked Ed to pick you up and bring you to his place. Dad and I jumped in the car and headed over there. When we arrived, we picked you up, and not one word was spoken in the car. I stopped at Mom's grave and told you to go see your mother."

At that time in my life, I was carrying so much guilt. I had led my family into a multi-level marketing business, Equinox, that financially devastated us all. I felt responsible. After that, I had moved in with a friend, Larry, and my drug addiction only worsened. I don't blame Larry at all; we were both too much alike—high energy, lovers of partying, impulsive. Eventually, I moved back to Texas to escape the environment I was in, but my addiction followed me.

I got married, had a child, and lost my mom, but I still couldn't shake the grip of my crack addiction. That night, while waiting for Mike and Ed to pick me up, I had hit rock bottom. I was a wreck, still wearing the tuxedo from the wedding, reeking of booze and sweat. Ed told me later that when he found me, I was leaning against a telephone pole in one of the worst neighborhoods in town.

I knew I'd be facing Mike, Dad, and the rest of my family—the very people I had hurt most with the Equinox disaster and my addiction. That drive to meet them might have been the longest, most painful drive of my life. When we got close to the cemetery, Mike didn't ask if I wanted to go see Mom's grave—he just told me. I had no choice.

I got out of the car and walked toward Mom's grave, my legs shaking, tears already streaming down my face. When I reached her stone, I fell to my knees in front of it, overcome with guilt and remorse, and I just sobbed. I had caused her so much pain, even if she hadn't known the full extent of my struggles. I had let her down.

My mom was a prayer warrior. She prayed for everyone she knew, for the world, for peace, for everything. Somehow, over the years, she had sensed I was in deep trouble, and she had fasted, prayed, and sat for hours in front of the Blessed Sacrament, interceding for me. I knew in my heart that she could hear me as I knelt there, begging for her forgiveness.

After what felt like hours, something shifted in me. It wasn't like all the guilt and pain suddenly disappeared, but I felt an unexpected sense of peace wash over me. In that moment, I knew I had to face my demons fully and make real changes in my life. With God's grace, my mother's prayers, and the support of others, I'm happy to say that I found my purpose.

I am an addict in recovery. Once an addict, always an addict. I've learned that addiction is a disease, and my brain has been permanently altered by the years of drug and alcohol abuse. But every day, I rely on the strength and grace I find in God, given to me, in confession and Mass, to maintain my sobriety. So far, so good.

## From the Crack House to God's House

On December 28th, 2006, my last child was born—my son, Layton Layne Francis. Because of homeschooling, coaching, and working out together, we've spent more time together in his first 17 years than many fathers are privileged to spend with their sons in a lifetime. The verdict on how everything turns out is still pending, but as I write this, the world and all its temptations seem to have my youngest boy in their sights. Over the past 15 years, people have often told me, "Tim, you must face some serious spiritual attacks because of all the effort you've put into promoting the fight against evil." My answer is always the same: "Absolutely. The enemy wants to divide families. A house divided cannot stand."

Please pray for me and my family. Layton and I are wrapping up our final year of football together, and then we move on to the next chapter of life.

**Layton through the years:**

### Mom was still working on the other side

In the spring of 2009, Pk and I had been married for almost ten years and were raising our three kids. At that time, we were still attending both the non-denominational church and Catholic Mass as a compromise. My kids, of course, loved the non-denominational church with all its fun activities, and they considered Catholic Mass more of a chore, almost like a jail sentence. At one point, Pk asked if I could keep statues of Mary and Marian prayers out of the house. That request, of course, came from the teachings of the "Bible-only" churches we had been attending.

Then, something miraculous happened. An old friend, Damon Stone, called me out of the blue and said, "Hey Tim, you left some tapes at my house years ago. I figured you might want them back." We met up, and when he handed me the tapes, guess what was in there? The VCR tape my mom had made of the woman experiencing the stigmata on the show *Signs from God – Science Tests Faith*. I had thought I'd lost that tape years ago. If you remember, I had called the TV station and even reached out to the priest featured in the show, but there was no further information available—no website, no book, nothing. I'd always wanted to know more about it. Was it real? What did it mean?

In 2009, I searched the Internet again and stumbled upon a website promoting a book called *Reason to Believe* by Ron Tesoriero. The promotional material said things like:

- A statue weeps and bleeds.
- A grandmother receives the stigmata.
- God dictates messages and teachings.
- A piece of bread changes to flesh.
- Are these claims true?
- What does science have to say?

The promo explained that this book was the fascinating journey of an Australian lawyer, Ron Tesoriero, who set out to find answers. He invited Mike Willesee, a highly respected investigative journalist, to join him in the journey. What they discovered, it said, would challenge the mind and heart of every reader.

Wow! This was so much more than I had ever imagined. Until then, the only supernatural thing I knew of was the woman experiencing the stigmata. Now, I was hearing about a weeping, bleeding statue and a piece of bread that had turned into flesh. And the fact that a lawyer and a respected journalist were investigating these claims, using science to determine the truth, was the cherry on top.

On March 10th, 2009, I ordered the book *Reason to Believe* along with two DVDs—*A Plea to Humanity* and *The Eucharist in Communion With Me*. Ron's assistant, Lyn, expedited them to me from Australia.

Reading the book and watching the DVDs absolutely blew my mind! I saw raw footage that Ron himself had filmed of Catalina Rivas experiencing two stigmatas. I saw videos and photos of the statue of Jesus crying and bleeding, and I witnessed the footage of the communion host turning into flesh and blood. It was overwhelming!

Around this time, after discovering Ron's work, I started reading the book aloud to Pk whenever we had the chance. Gradually, she became as convinced as I was that the Catholic faith was the one true faith. Without ever having a big discussion about it, we just stopped attending Fellowship Church.

Since then, Ron Tesoriero has written two more books. His most recent one, *My Human Heart*, covers over 20 years of research and results. There is a massive amount of incredible information that I don't have the time or expertise to cover here, but I will say this: the bleeding statue of Jesus, the communion hosts that have turned into human heart tissue, and the stigmata are signs that lead people back to the sacraments and devotions of the ancient Christians. The

MOVING FORWARD

highest gift is Jesus Christ offering Himself as the sacrificial lamb in the Holy Sacrifice of the Mass.

The following are three photos that Ron has given me permission to share—pictures he took himself:

*Statue as purchased by owner*

*In 1995 the statue is filmed weeping and bleeding*

133

## From the Crack House to God's House

*On 18 August 1996 Padre Alezandro Pezet found an abandoned Communion host in his church after Mass. He placed it in a bowl of water and locked it in the tabernacle.*

*On 26 August 1996, when the tabernacle was opened, he noticed that a red substance was coming from the host.*

As I read and watched everything with rapt attention, I kept asking myself, "How have I never heard of these things before?" I knew deep down that what I was seeing and learning was beyond extraordinary. Mike Willesee and Ron Tesoriero's reputations were impeccable, making what I was encountering even more credible.

I was utterly amazed by the revelations in the materials from Australia. Let me walk you through some of what I learned...

## The Stigmata

Let me remind you that when, a person mysteriously manifests the wounds of Jesus Christ during His crucifixion. Though rare, these phenomena have appeared intermittently throughout the last two millennia.

Stigmata wounds typically appear on the forehead, hands, feet, and side, and the recipient often struggles with intense breathing difficulties, much like Jesus did on the cross.

The Fox TV Special, *Signs from God*, was the first time a person was filmed before, during, and after receiving the stigmata. The special was a significant success, with 29 million people watching it across North America. Yet despite this, you'd be hard-pressed to find one in a hundred thousand Americans who are familiar with it. I would even go as far as to say that perhaps only one in several hundred million people know the details of what truly transpired before, during, and after that event.

The words of New Zealand journalist Alastair Thompson resonate deeply when he discussed this supernatural occurrence:

> "Put it this way – this is either the biggest hoax of the 20th century, in which case it would have to be a fairly huge conspiracy, or the most important moment of the century, if not the whole millennium."

Through a great deal of research and evidence, Ron Tesoriero, the attorney, concluded that Catalina Rivas was an authentic mystic. He said, "The world, I felt, should know that the stigmata is real, factual in every way, perhaps more real than much of what passes for news in our media. I didn't want to tell people what was happening—I wanted them to see it for themselves."

Thankfully, the "skeptical" Mike Willesee accepted Ron's challenge to "prove me wrong" about Catalina's stigmata being real. Watching this one event ended up changing the lives of my family forever. The most astonishing thing is that the harshest criticism you can find online about her stigmata is that she somehow cut herself without anyone noticing!

After watching the TV broadcast thousands of times, reviewing the raw footage filmed by Ron, and seeing Mike Willesee's impeccable credentials, I find it both ignorant and disingenuous for anyone to claim otherwise. You can judge for yourself by watching the footage on the website: www.ScienceTestsFaith.com.

Ron emphasized, "There were at least nine people in the room who witnessed Katya experience the stigmata that day: Mike Willesee, myself, Greg Barbara (an Australian 60 Minutes cameraman), his sound recorder, Ralph Steele (a neuropsychophysiologist), Dr. Ricardo Castanon, and others. Yet critics who claim this was a hoax haven't asked to see the raw footage or speak to any of the nine witnesses."

And let's not forget—if they believe she somehow inflicted those wounds herself or had help from someone else, how do they explain how the wounds completely healed overnight, leaving no trace?

As I wrote earlier, a quick Google search for "famous stigmatists" will reveal just how many documented cases there are. For instance, Saint Padre Pio bled from the stigmata for 50 years.

I also learned about "incorruptibility," a phenomenon where a corpse miraculously avoids decomposition. One of the most famous cases is that of St. Bernadette. Her coffin was opened after thirty years in the grave, and her body was found in a state of perfect preservation. Her incorrupt body lies in a glass shrine at the chapel of the convent of Saint-Gildard in Nevers, France, and remains intact to this day.

Why hadn't I heard about these things before? I grew up Catholic, but no one had ever shared this information with me.

1 Corinthians 15:52-53 says, "For the trumpet will sound, the dead will be raised incorruptible, and we shall be changed, for that which is corruptible must clothe itself with incorruptibility, and that which is mortal must clothe itself with immortality." The incorruptible bodies of saints are examples of what the Church calls motives of credibility, showing that faith is not "a blind impulse of the mind" (Catechism 156).

Reading Ron's book, I was astonished to learn about *Our Lady of Guadalupe*. The feast of Our Lady of Guadalupe dates back to the 16th century. A poor Indian was baptized and given the name Juan Diego. He was a 57-year-old widower and lived in a small village near Mexico City. On Saturday morning, December 9, 1531, he was on his way to a nearby barrio to attend Mass in honor of Our Lady. Juan was walking by a hill called Tepeyac when he heard beautiful music, like the warbling of birds. A radiant cloud appeared, and within it stood an Indian maiden dressed like an Aztec princess. The lady spoke to him in his own language and sent him to the Bishop of Mexico, a Franciscan named Juan de Zumarraga. The Bishop was to build a chapel in the place where the Lady appeared. Eventually, the Bishop told Juan to have the lady give him a sign. At about this same time, Juan's uncle became seriously ill. This led poor Juan to try to avoid the Lady. Nevertheless. the lady found Juan, assured him that his uncle would recover, and provided roses for Juan to carry to the Bishop in his cape or tilma. On December 12, when Juan Diego opened his tilma in the Bishop's presence, the roses fell to the ground, and the Bishop sank to his knees. On the inside of tilma, where the roses had been, appeared an image of Mary exactly as she had appeared at the hill of Tepeyac.

In recent years, scientific studies of the image on the tilma, still remarkably preserved, have revealed several unusual properties:

1. Iridescence: The colors change depending on the viewing angle, a phenomenon that cannot be reproduced by hand.

2. No Paint Residue: Tests show no evidence of paint or dye on the tilma, and the colors are not from any known natural or mineral substances.

3. No Brush Strokes: Microscopic analysis reveals no brush strokes, as though the image appeared in a single moment.

4. Smooth Texture: According to Kodak of Mexico, the image feels like a modern photograph, even though it was created centuries before photography.

5. Reflected Images: The eyes of the Virgin reflect images, including that of Juan Diego, and they react like human eyes when exposed to light.

6. Temperature: Regardless of its environment, the tilma maintains a constant temperature of 98.6°F, the temperature of a human body.

I quote Ron Tesoriero from *Reason to Believe*:

> "NASA researchers Smith and Callahan, using infrared photography, began a study on Our Lady of Guadalupe in May 1979. Callahan concludes: 'For those who do not believe in miracles, my only solution is to end my study with the words of G.K. Chesterton: My belief in miracles is founded on human evidence, just as my belief in the discovery of America is.'
>
> "It is, indeed, a simple logical fact that hardly needs to be recognized or interpreted. The extraordinary idea going around is that those who deny the miracle know how to consider the facts coolly and directly, while those who accept the miracle always relate the facts with the dogma previously accepted. In fact, the opposite is the case: the believers accept the miracle (with or without reason) because the evidence compels them to do so. The unbelievers deny it (with or without reason) because the doctrine they profess compels them to do so."

## The image as it appeared on Juan Diego's Tilma:

## The Shroud of Turin

A large cloth known as the "Shroud of Turin" has been closely examined for decades. Many believe it's the burial cloth that was wrapped around Jesus after His crucifixion, and studies seem to confirm its authenticity. For more information on this, I highly recommend googling "Shroud of Turin — Fr. Andrew Dalton." If you're interested in how the Church investigates the supernatural, check out my friend Michael O'Neill's book, *Science and the Miraculous*.

In my earlier studies of ancient Christian faith, I had mostly focused on the biblical and historical teachings. But now, I was discovering all these supernatural events that had been validated by science. This was a new and thrilling path for me.

## Signs Point to Something

When you're driving, signs always point to something, guiding you in the right direction. The stigmata was clearly a "Sign from God," but the question was—what was this sign pointing to? When I first saw the video of the stigmata, I had three important questions:

1. Is it real?
2. Is it from God?
3. What is its message for me?

## Is It Real?

The only way to prove something is real is by looking at the evidence and judging its likelihood. None of us have met George Washington, but we believe in his existence because of historical documents and credible witnesses. It's the same way we approach the stigmata:

- Film footage of Catalina experiencing multiple stigmata, captured from different camera angles
- Credible witnesses present at the scene
- Stigmata has been documented worldwide for centuries

## Is It From God?

- The woman who received the stigmata, Catalina Rivas, was filmed while receiving messages she claims are from Jesus Christ.
- As history shows, Jesus established a Church.
- The Catholic Church is the only one that can trace its beginnings directly back to Jesus.
- Catalina's messages have been reviewed by her bishop and theologians and found to align with the teachings of the Church.

On page 56 of *My Human Heart*, Ron Tesoriero asked Fr. Omar Huesca (a priest and psychologist) about the authenticity of Catalina's experiences:

**Ron:** "Some say Catalina's experiences could come from the dark side, not from God. What do you think?"

**Fr. Omar:** "I don't believe that. Her experiences have led to edification and conversion—not just for herself, but for others. This echoes what happened with Christ. People accused Him of casting out demons with the power of Satan. Jesus responded, 'How can Satan cast out Satan? A house divided cannot stand.' I believe that the adage 'By their fruits, you will know them' is crucial here. Catalina's experiences have brought people to Christ, and that's why I find it hard to believe this could be from Satan."

## What's the Message for Me? (My "Takeaway")

After diving deep into Ron's and Mike's investigation of Catalina's stigmata, reading all her messages, and reflecting on my 20 years of learning the Church's teachings, here are my key takeaways:

- Many people have turned away from God, forgetting the suffering Jesus endured for their sake. Jesus used Catalina's suffering to remind the world of His own suffering, especially through someone who had drifted away from Him.

- Jesus is always waiting for us to return to Him. He is patient and merciful, welcoming everyone back with open arms and open hearts.

- Jesus wants to unite His heart with ours, offering His love to the world. We receive this offer through the Holy Eucharist at Mass.

- Jesus is truly present in the Eucharist after the priest consecrates the host. When He says, "Unless you eat the flesh of the Son of Man and drink His blood, you have no life in you," He means a spiritual union. Think of it like melting two candles into one; we are united with Christ in a profound way through Communion.

- The Eucharist is "The Bread of Life" that nourishes and strengthens the soul, just as regular food sustains our bodies.

- Holy Communion preserves and increases the supernatural life of the soul, repairing and building spiritual strength.

- Catalina received the stigmata on the first Friday of the Sacred Heart devotion. The Sacred Heart of Jesus, celebrated in the Eucharist, is the key to healing the pain, division, and suffering in the world.

- If your soul is damaged through serious sin, the Sacrament of Confession restores it.
- Confession is like medicine for the soul—it repels temptations, cures vices, destroys Satan's influence, and provides grace and virtue.
- Suffering, when united with Christ's passion, takes on new meaning. It becomes part of His saving work for humanity.

### Eucharistic Miracles

Over the 2000+ years since Jesus' resurrection, there have been hundreds of documented Eucharistic miracles. Many believe that just as Jesus used signs and miracles to attract His followers and prove His divinity, He is still doing that today. If you google "Eucharistic Miracles," you will see dozens of documented cases in which the communion host has turned into flesh and blood of living heart tissue.

Of the thousands of Eucharistic miracles, one which occurred relatively recently happened in Buenos Aires in 1996. A parishioner approached a priest after Mass and told him that someone had put a consecrated host in a candle stick at the back of the Church. A consecrated host is a wafer of bread upon which the priest says the words of Jesus: "This is my body." At that moment, the ancient Christians believed, and Catholics teach today, exactly what Justin Martyr said in 151 A.D:

> "For not as common bread nor common drink do we receive these; but since Jesus Christ our Savior was made incarnate by the word of God and had both flesh and blood for our salvation, so too, as we have

been taught, the food which has been made into the Eucharist by the Eucharistic prayer set down by him, and by the change of which our blood and flesh is nurtured, is both the flesh and the blood of that incarnated Jesus."

Every Catholic Church in the world has a special sink that is piped directly into the earth, not into a septic system, sewer, or well. When something like this happens, the priest is instructed to place the defiled host in a bowl of Holy Water and lock it in the Tabernacle (a depository in every Catholic Church that holds unused consecrated hosts). Typically, when the priest returns in a day or two, the host will have dissolved into the Holy Water, and then the priest will pour it down that special drain directly into the earth.

In this case, when the priest returned to the Tabernacle, expecting to see the host dissolved, it appeared that something resembling flesh and blood had grown on it. The priest locked it back in the Tabernacle. Months went by, and it continued to sit in the Tabernacle.

After sitting in water for over three years, Cardinal Bergoglio of the Buenos Aires area (now Pope Francis) agreed to have the substance tested. He directed the testing to be carried out under the most scrupulous conditions. Subsequently, with witnesses and cameras filming the process, small amounts were taken off the host and placed in three test tubes. The samples were examined by eight scientists from three continents.

The results were mind-blowing – that the substance that had grown on a consecrated host was heart tissue from the left ventricle of a heart that had been severely tortured. They were amazed that there were living white blood cells still in the substance, amazed because when living tissue is removed from the body that has white blood cells, they live no longer than one hour and usually die immediately. To say that the labs were astonished is an understatement. There is simply no reason other than divine interference for the consecrated host to morph into living heart tissue. Again, I encourage you to google this to learn more about the numerous Eucharistic miracles that have been documented. By the power of my mother's prayers, I was put in direct contact with the very man who led the investigation into multiple Eucharistic Miracles, Ron Tesoriero. I have barely scratched the surface of these miracles. Wait until you read his book, *My Human Heart*. The blood test results will blow you away! After reading it, you can thank my mother, Patricia Ann Francis.

At the end of the TV Prime Time Special, *Signs from God-Science Tests Faith*, Mike Willesee asked Catalina Rivas if she had a message from Jesus after having suffered the stigmata. Here is the message that Catalina says was from Jesus to the world:

> "Dear men of the 20th Century. You have forgotten Me. I will be coming back again to take you away from the darkness and show you true faith. I come to hug you. I want to put My Heart next to your heart. To transmit My love to all humanity. Do you want to hug Me? Your souls are as delicate as a rose petal. Let Me impress in it, My love." (Jesus to Catalina)

Amazing! Jesus says he wants to impress His love into our souls. What is the symbol for love? The heart! When you google "Eucharistic Miracles," you find that over and over again, the host is turned into a Human Heart. I highly recommend that you read Ron Tesoriero's book *My Human Heart*. If you live in North America, then go to www.ScienceTestsFaith.com for the cheapest and fastest way to get this book.

Regarding the "messages" of Catalina Rivas (Stigmatist):

- She has a seventh-grade education with no theological training. She has written over eighty books. At times, she has written in Greek, Polish, and Latin. These are languages she cannot read, write, or speak.

- Ron Tesoriero filmed her writing for almost one hour without pausing. Quoting Ron: "She started with a blank page in her notebook. She wrote the first sentence and without stopping, the next sentence, then paragraph after paragraph, and then page after page, without one pause. She did not refer to any other material or book to write those 14 pages.

- Catalina's Archbishop said, "We have read Catalina's books, and we are certain that their only objective is to lead us all on a journey of authentic spirituality that is based on the Gospel of Christ. I authorize their printing and distribution and recommend them as texts of meditation and spiritual orientation in order to yield much fruit for Our Lord, who is calling us to save many souls, showing us that He is a living God, full of love and mercy."

- The Church does NOT put her messages on the same level as the Word of God (Written & Oral). They are not meant to compete with The Word of God. They are meant to complement the Word of God in the same way that a good book or sermon does.

- To learn more about these approved books and, hopefully, read some of them, go to *www.ScienceTestsFaith.com* and click on the "Books" tab.

### What to do?

After reading the book *Reason to Believe*, watching the DVDs A Plea to Humanity and The Eucharist in Communion with Me, and delving into the messages from Catalina Rivas, I was completely overwhelmed by a deep sense of belief and conviction. I made a commitment to immerse myself more fully in the sacramental and devotional practices of the ancient Christians—frequent confession, daily Mass, the rosary, holy hours, and reading the Bible with the understanding of the time it was written. But then came the big question: what was I going to do with all this newfound information?

I felt a stirring deep within my soul. Maybe my natural ability to speak and persuade could be used to share this message with others. But the thought of putting myself out there was both humbling and terrifying. Who was I to share Christ's teachings? After all, for most of my adult life, I had been a slave to vice, living the "carpe diem" lifestyle—seize the day, because you only live once, right?

Then I thought of Catalina Rivas. She was a party girl, married and divorced three times, and had been a mistress to a powerful government official. In one of her messages, she asked the Lord why He chose her. His reply was, "You ask Me why. Once more I repeat, I came to save sinners. What merit would it have, if in these times, a virtuous person should speak for me? It is as if a rich person would offer a plate of soup—nothing new. But that same plate in the hands of a beggar would be a miracle of love worthy of thanks."

That message struck me deeply. Maybe my own brokenness made me the perfect person to share Jesus' message. If I truly believed everything I had learned, I had an obligation to share it, no matter my past.

Reading Catalina's messages also helped me answer

another pressing question. If the Catholic Church really is the one Jesus established—if He offers Himself as the sacrificial Lamb at every Mass, and if participating in this sacrifice allows us to "eat His flesh and drink His blood" so that He abides in us—then why weren't Catholics showing up in droves for daily Mass?

It baffled me. Why did the non-denominational mega-churches seem more passionate about Jesus and salvation? I wasn't trying to be rude, but I couldn't help noticing that at Catholic Mass, people often came late and left early. Meanwhile, at the mega-churches, people arrived early, stayed late, and were involved in countless small groups and Bible studies.

A bit of research revealed that many Catholics who left for non-denominational churches did so because they didn't feel "fed" in the Catholic Church. Even more shocking, over 70% of Catholics registered at parishes didn't believe in the Real Presence of Jesus—body, blood, soul, and divinity—in the Eucharist. These aren't people who left the Church; they're registered members. But here's the problem: you can't be a Catholic in good standing and not believe in this central teaching. It's like saying, "I'm alive, but I just don't breathe!"

I'm not condemning anyone for this. In fact, I find it exciting. It's like discovering the best-kept secret in the world and having the privilege to share it. If only people knew the truth about the Eucharist and the Mass, might they return with open hearts and deep faith?

Then I read a message from Jesus to Catalina that brought everything into focus: "You do not know how holy, how misunderstood and how maltreated is that unique Sacrament in which I give Myself to you. That is the reason for these books, because a large part of the laity in My Church are ignorant of so many things that for the other part are common and even ordinary."

Catalina also wrote, "What a pity for those persons who receive the Lord in a humdrum routine manner, without the wonder of telling Jesus something new, but always using the same tiresome words, or even worse, not saying anything to Him, or feeling anything, as if they were actually receiving just a piece of bread."

Jesus added, "How can you possibly be surprised at the laity if the majority of them are scarcely aware of My Presence in the Eucharist, and are just beginning to believe that I am here alive. How can you possibly be surprised if on many occasions I prove in My own brothers and sisters, that the lessons I have tried to give them through so many Eucharistic Miracles have rolled right off their souls without penetrating them."

It became crystal clear—most Catholics, like me, were simply ignorant. Many of us grew up in the faith because our parents took us to church, but we never fully embraced or understood what we were receiving. Meanwhile, the mega-churches were connecting with people on a cultural level, with music that sounded familiar, modern styles, and no vulgarity. They made church fun and relatable. I don't fault them for that—it's smart. If I had gone to a non-Catholic seminary, I'd believe what they believe, too.

I don't regret moving from the "bar scene" to the "Bible scene" with the non-denominational church. It was a necessary stepping stone in my search for the truth. But I'm disappointed that they teach things that contradict God's Word—things no Christian believed or taught for over 1500 years after Christ.

The story of Jesus is not some Santa Claus or Tooth Fairy tale. It's rooted in historical evidence, and that evidence overwhelmingly points to the ancient Christians being, well, Catholic. As Cardinal Newman, a famous Protestant historian who became Catholic, said: "To be deep in history is to cease to be a Protestant."

That's why over 1,200 non-Catholic Christian pastors have left their churches to become lay Catholics in the last 25 years. I have never heard of a committed Catholic researching their way into the non-denominational church. But I've heard many stories of people like me, who didn't fully embrace or understand their Catholic faith, finding the mega-churches more appealing.

How many times have I heard, "I didn't have a personal relationship with Jesus until I came to XYZ Bible Church?" I don't doubt their sincerity. But it doesn't get more personal than receiving Jesus Himself in the Eucharist.

I want to be very clear: the Catholic Church does not teach, nor do I believe, that people who aren't Catholic are bad or going to hell. My message is simply this…

1. Jesus Christ is a real person from history who was crucified and rose from the dead.

2. Jesus Christ established a Church.

3. This Church was given some amazing supernatural gifts called the Sacraments. These Sacraments can heal wounds caused by the world and the flesh. These gifts are waiting for anyone wanting to be healed and protected from evil.

4. God can work outside of the Sacraments in the Catholic Church. However, these are the normative means that Jesus established and left to convey grace into our souls. Take advantage of them!

5. If you are a non-Catholic pastor, I would very much like to talk to you about how we can work together to heal our family, country, and world. Please contact me.

Over time, it became painfully clear to me that many Catholics are completely unaware of the incredible treasures Christ has given us through His Church: the seven sacraments and a rich devotional life. They just need to be "awakened" like I was. On the other hand, non-Catholic Christians, especially those in the mega-churches, are often taught that all they need is a personal relationship with Jesus and to follow the Bible as best as they can. And from my experience, they do an amazing job of that. But here's the thing—they don't know what they're missing by not partaking in the Eucharist, by not "eating His flesh and drinking His blood." And, from what I've seen, they're often not particularly interested in hearing about it either.

I eventually managed to get in touch with Ron Tesoriero, the author of *Reason to Believe*, all the way in Australia. We set up a call to discuss all the ideas I had swirling in my head. When I pursue something, I don't think small—go big or go home, right? I had these grand visions of organizing events across the United States to showcase the incredible story Ron shares in his book. I wanted to get him on every major platform—Larry King, Oprah, and Piers Morgan—you name it. I was, and still am, convinced that if millions of people read *Reason to Believe*, there would be millions more opening their hearts to the treasures of the Catholic Church, especially the gift of the Eucharist—not just for eternal life but for the fruits of the Spirit here on Earth.

I've seen the dark side. I've stared evil in the face more times than I care to remember. I know what it's like to live without the sacraments, and I know the grace that comes from receiving them. As much as I love Ron's original book, *Reason to Believe*, I highly recommend his latest work, *My Human Heart*, which includes all the updated findings from his scientific investigations into supernatural occurrences—stuff that so few people know about.

Ron, however, is not like me. He's incredibly detail-oriented, thorough, and methodical. He moves very slowly, and I respect that. But it drove me crazy that he wasn't interested in taking his story to huge platforms. Instead, he's focused on completing the next phase of his research into Eucharistic miracles. That said, he did have a burning desire to show the world the truth of Catalina Rivas' stigmata, which is why he challenged Mike Willesee to prove it false. That challenge eventually led to the *Signs from God* TV special, which aired to 29 million people in 1999.

Looking back, I can't help but wonder what would have happened if Ron's book had been available right after that special aired. If 10% of the viewers had bought the book, that's 2.9 million people who would have been exposed to a massive amount of evidence—a true *Reason to Believe*. Think about it: Rick Warren's *A Purpose Driven Life* has sold 50 million copies, and that's just one man's take on living a purpose-driven life. Nothing against Rick Warren or his book, but what Ron's research uncovers is infinitely more valuable, in my opinion. If 50 million people read Ron's book, Catholic Mass attendance would skyrocket, and that kind of revival could lead to less division in our families, our country, and our world.

### Enter Bob Hughes.

Ron put me in touch with Bob Hughes, a successful business owner in the United States who was helping to publish and promote *Reason to Believe*. Bob had initially been skeptical about the apparitions of the Virgin Mary in Medjugorje, but when he visited in 1989, he had several miraculous experiences that changed him into a devout, on-fire Catholic. Below are some pictures and descriptions of miraculous occurrences Bob witnessed during his time there.

Bob's experiences remind me of something my mom once wrote to me:

> "Three days before the feast of Pentecost are a special time. We need to spend time in prayer to the Holy Spirit. The Feast of Pentecost is this Sunday. You

need to give the Lord a chance to talk to you. You need a quiet, empty mind."

I have included reports in Bob's own words, detailing what happened during his time at the site of Mary's apparitions, along with photos that clearly depict something miraculous. One of the photos is of a cross at the exact spot where Mary appeared, and when it was developed, the image revealed something truly extraordinary.

> This is one of many "Normal Pictures" taken at night in Medjugorje, Yugoslavia, in March 1989. It is similar to what we saw while taking any of the pictures that night with our 35mm camera. We did not see anything like it in the Miraculous Picture! We only saw it when we returned home and developed the film.
>
> As you can see, there were people praying around. In the "Miraculous Picture", you can see two heads at the bottom center. These were people that were there. Notice that there is a "tongue of fire" on top of their head, but no Dove formation is coming from it. Perhaps this is what the "Tongues of Fire" really looked like when Tongues of Fire rested on top of the heads of the Apostles during Pentecost.
>
> In the "Normal Picture," you see the medal cross. In the "Miraculous Picture," you can see how the crossbar changes to wood-like except at the very beginning on the left side.
>
> If this picture has become separated from the "Miraculous Picture," you made, request a copy of the Miraculous Picture by sending your request to:
>
> R.J. Hughes, P.O. Box 1160, Hampstead, NC 28443
>
> Please visit the Medjugorje website for more info at: www.medjugorje.ws

## The Most Holy Trinity

Dear Brothers and Sisters in Christ, I share this Miraculous picture with you that God has given to me to strengthen my weak faith and change my worldly ways. I pray that God, in His Love and Mercy, will also touch your heart and strengthen your faith as He did mine as I humbly try to Bear Witness to you.

This Miraculous picture was taken on the Holy Saturday night, March 25, 1989, at the site of the first apparition of the Blessed Virgin Mary in Medjugorje, Yugoslavia. What is seen in this picture was not visible to the naked eye and was only discovered after the film was developed upon our return home to the USA. I was there and had the original untouched negative and other "normal" pictures taken that night, like the one included here.

Concerning this picture, the Holy Spirit is clearly seen in the form of a Dove Head. There are a total of seven Dove Heads coming from tongues of fire. Perhaps this represents the Seven Gifts of the Holy Spirit. God the Father and God the Son are located in the center of Dove's head. About half of the suffering face of Jesus with a crown of thorns is in the top middle of the center Dove head. God the Father is immediately below the face of Jesus at a slight angle. He looks like "old man winter" with ruffled hair, heavy eyebrows & puffy cheeks. If you have difficulty in locating God the Father or God the Son, please use the drawing I made to help locate the Holy Trinity. If you do not have a "normal" picture to compare or a drawing, please write it down, and I will be glad to send you one for free.

I share this event with you for what it is worth to

# FROM THE CRACK HOUSE TO GOD'S HOUSE

you. In 1989, I was always sort of a "Doubting Thomas" who said, "Show me." These two pictures, Miraculous and Normal, show me God's great Love and Mercy towards another "Doubting Thomas." It has strengthened my faith greatly, and I know without a doubt that God does exist! I am still a sinner, but my conversion continues each day. God's Grace continues to strengthen me and lead me in His ways as presented in the Bible and the traditions and teachings of the Holy Catholic Church. Please visit the Medjugorje Web Site: www.medjugorje.ws

I share this gift freely with you as it was freely given to me by God to strengthen my weak faith and trust in Him. For more information, please write to: R.J. Hughes, P.O. Box 1160, Hampstead, NC 28443.

**Normal Picture:**

### Miraculous Picture:

After experiencing the miraculous, Bob Hughes was so moved that he considered selling his successful ceramic and tile distributorship, which generated nearly $10 million in annual revenue, and giving the proceeds to the poor. He consulted a priest, who advised him that while there would always be poor people to help, Bob's resources could be better used in another way—by showing people that God is real. So, Bob focused his energy on using his resources to lead young people to Medjugorje, where they could witness signs and wonders beyond human ability.

Bob and his wife Bernie also learned of the "Miracle of the Sun," which took place in Fatima, Portugal, on October 13, 1917. The Blessed Mother had appeared several times to three children, but no one believed their accounts—not even their families or the local priest. So, Mary promised that on a specific day, there would be a sign that would prove the children were telling the truth. Word spread, and up to 80,000 people gathered in a meadow where Mary had appeared. It was a dark, rainy day, but suddenly, the clouds parted, the rain stopped, and the sun seemed to grow larger, almost as if it was falling toward the earth. The sun appeared to dance in the sky. People panicked, fearing the end of the world, but then the sun returned to its normal place in the sky. Over 80,000 people, including atheists and journalists, witnessed the event.

The messages from the Blessed Mother, both at Medjugorje and Fatima, emphasized love for one's neighbor, peace in the world, and a plea for people to return to her Son, Jesus. Fatima is a recognized and approved apparition by the Church, while Medjugorje is still ongoing.

Through a series of connections, Bob was introduced to Ron Tesoriero around the time Ron and Ricardo were investigating Catalina Rivas. Back then, I could only find a fax number on Ron's website, so I sent a letter via fax, explaining my whole story—how my mom had given me the VCR tape and how watching the stigmata had grabbed my attention. I also shared how it took me ten years to get my hands on Ron's book and Catalina Rivas' messages. I felt a calling to help make more people aware of the gifts so few were taking advantage of—Confession, Mass, Adoration, the Rosary, and more. Bob called me and decided to send me a couple of cases of Ron's *Reason to Believe* books.

On June 10, 2009, I emailed Bob with a detailed outline of how we could share Ron and Mike's work with the world, using every available communication method. Then, on June 28, 2009, Ron emailed both Bob and me:

"As I mentioned in my earlier email, Mike and I are planning to come through the USA on our way back from Bolivia. The dates look like being 8th, 9th, and perhaps the 10th of September. Do you think you and Tim could arrange for us to give two talks on those days? If so, which city would they be in? We could also use this opportunity to discuss your ideas for evangelization."

I had never organized a church event before, so I was a bit naïve about how receptive Catholic priests and bishops would be. I thought churches would be eager to host Ron and Mike to share their story, especially since it had been featured in the two-hour documentary *Signs from God*. But I was wrong! Many priests seemed uncomfortable with the idea of anything supernatural. Looking back, I understand their caution. The Church is slow and deliberate in approving such events, wary of tricks or diabolical interference. But at the time, I was moving fast and full of excitement!

Even so, there's a big difference between skepticism and being closed-minded. The evidence Ron presents is overwhelming. As an attorney, he has built an airtight case.

As you can see from Ron's email, he simply mentioned the potential dates—September 8th, 9th, and 10th—for presentations in the U.S. Even though I lived in Texas, I felt a deep need to host the first event in Ohio to honor my mother. She had orchestrated this entire journey, both when she was alive and after she passed. I didn't realize it at the time, but September 8th is the Blessed Mother's birthday. I didn't plan for it, but looking back, I see it as divine timing.

When we finally reviewed the footage from the event, something stood out. You'll notice in the picture below that it looks like Mary, the Mother of God, is blessing Mike Willesee while he's speaking. Now, I know it's a statue of the Blessed Mother, but in all my years of attending Catholic churches, I've only seen a handful that have a statue of Mary

FROM THE CRACK HOUSE TO GOD'S HOUSE

directly behind the speaker's podium. I later found out that on September 8, 1993, Catalina Rivas had her first experience receiving a message from the Mother of God.

So, here I was, organizing an event to honor my mother on the Blessed Mother's birthday. People have told me this is a "signal grace," a visible sign that the event was being blessed. Catalina Rivas received this message from Jesus: "If one of your loved ones is far away from us. Pray for him. Give him to My Mother and She will bring him in Her arms to Me."

I truly believe that all of this—this journey of faith, these miraculous events—was brought about by the power of my mother's prayers. She prayed the Rosary daily, blessed each of us with Holy Water, even when we were thousands of miles away, and offered up our souls to Jesus at every Mass. The Bible says that with enough faith, you can move mountains, but without love, it's all meaningless. My mother, with her enormous heart and faith, embodied that love for everyone.

Below is the picture I'm referring to, showing Mike Willesee speaking at the Church of the Transfiguration in West Milton, Ohio, thanks to Fr. John MacQuarrie:

Thank God for Fr. John MacQuarrie, who graciously opened his parish for the presentation on the Blessed Mother's birthday in 2009. Fr. John was a native of New Carlisle, Ohio, and my mother knew him well.

Two days after hosting Ron and Mike in Ohio, I had them speak at St. Elizabeth Ann Seton in Keller, Texas. Below is a newspaper article highlighting Mike's presentation there:

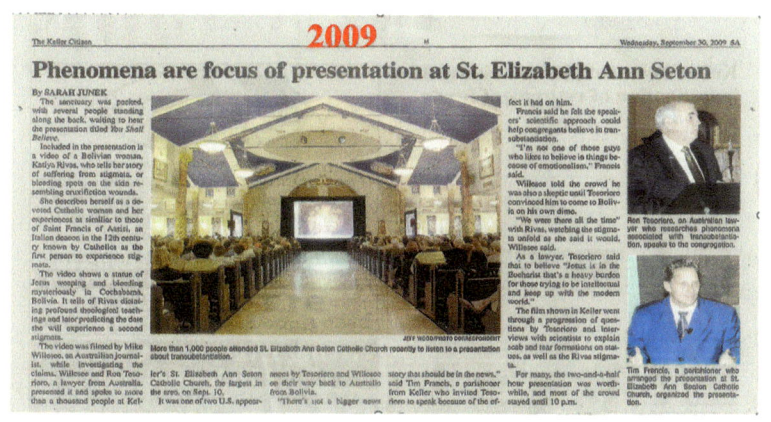

**Phenomena are focus of presentation at St. Elizabeth Ann Seton**

With standing-room-only crowds in Ohio and Texas, I was thrilled. It confirmed what I had suspected all along—I wasn't the only one asking, "Why haven't I ever heard of these things?"

Mike and Ron's presentations were hugely successful and resonated deeply with everyone who attended. This gave me even more confidence that my goals were realistic. I knew I wasn't alone in my fascination with the supernatural. I became more determined than ever to spread this story.

Now, this might sound crazy, but after hearing Ron and Mike speak, I realized there was so much more to our faith, so much more to the story, that they simply didn't have time to dive into during their talks. I had learned there were over 15,000 parishes in the United States, and 70% of registered Catholics miss Mass and don't believe in the Church's teaching that the bread and wine become the body and blood of Jesus Christ during consecration. At the same time, I kept hearing about something called "The New Evangelization," a movement started by St. Pope John Paul II. He called on Catholics to reach out to fallen-away Catholics using "new methods, new expressions, and new ardor."

Well, that's exactly what reached me! As I've shared, it all started with my mother sending me that VHS tape of a woman experiencing the stigmata. That grabbed my attention and made me want to know more. Unfortunately, it took ten years for me to get my hands on the message behind the miracle when I finally read Ron's book *Reason to Believe* and the messages from Jesus and Mary given through Catalina Rivas.

Jesus had told Catalina: "Look at your pen. For Me, you are my pen that I use to trace the symbols that express my words. What your hand writes, guided by mine, will remain. Repeated and amplified, it will fill the earth. What I need is to convey messages to humanity through you."

## A Signal Grace from Mom

Ten years after my mother had sent me that tape of *Signs from God-Science Tests Faith*, hosted by Mike Willesee, the father of investigative journalism in Australia, I found myself hosting the same Mike Willesee in Ohio—on the Blessed Mother's birthday, no less. Around that time, my daughter Hailey found a newspaper clipping that my mom had put in the local paper announcing our wedding in Lake

Tahoe. It was laminated, and when I turned it over, I couldn't believe what I saw on the reverse side.

Was it possible that my mom had somehow arranged this? Did she call the newspaper in 1999 and say, "My son is getting married outside of the Catholic Church. Can you place an ad on the reverse side, calling Catholics back to the Church, lining up perfectly with my son's wedding announcement?"

Fast forward ten years, and here I was hosting an event with the very same journalist who had filmed the stigmata, all with the goal of bringing lukewarm and fallen-away Catholics back home. Many holy Catholics have told me that the ad lining up with my wedding announcement was a "signal grace" from both my biological mother and our spiritual mother, the Blessed Mother. They were directing me to lead souls back to the path Jesus had paved.

## When It Rains, It Pours

Around that same time, things seemed to happen all at once. I was asked to do a recap presentation for the Seton Moms group at St. Elizabeth Ann Seton, where I had organized the previous talk. The leader of the group mentioned that several people had missed the original presentation, so I agreed to do it on October 27, 2009. In preparing, I wanted to create a PowerPoint presentation that not only included some of the things Ron and Mike had discussed but also summarized my ten-year journey back to the Catholic faith.

While attending daily Mass at St. Elizabeth, I noticed a kiosk at the back of the church with CDs from *Lighthouse Catholic Media*. You can now listen to many of them for free through FORMED, an adult education program offered by many parishes. If your parish doesn't have it, I highly recommend asking them to get it!

One CD, in particular, caught my eye:

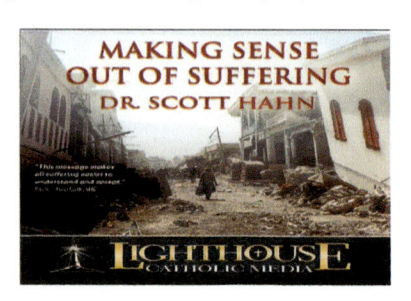

Millions of Catholics and non-denominational Christians alike have asked the same universal question: "Why does a loving God allow suffering?" There are even atheists and agnostics who argue that suffering proves there can't be a God. This misses the entire concept of redemptive suffering—a concept I'm convinced 98% of people have never been taught.

Through my studies, I learned about "victim souls" like St. Francis of Assisi, St. Padre Pio, St. Catherine of Siena, Rhoda Wise, and Theresa Neumann. I spent time with the very men who filmed a woman predicting and experiencing the stigmata, and I personally spent hours with that woman, Catalina Rivas. I also watched my mother take her last breath, leaving my father in Ohio to grieve her loss.

*Making Sense Out of Suffering* had my attention! In short, Dr. Scott Hahn, a theologian and former Protestant minister, made several key points on the CD:

- The main goal of the Holy Spirit is to produce in us Christ's life, death, suffering, and resurrection.
- We are all going to suffer, but if we unite our suffering with Christ's, it can be used to help others.
- In the Bible, Paul says, "In my flesh, I complete what is lacking in Christ's afflictions for the sake of the body, the Church." What's lacking in Christ's afflictions is our participation in His suffering.

- If we want to be resurrected with Christ, we must suffer with Him.

After hearing this, I immediately sent the CD to my brother Mike. I called him later and asked, "So, what did you think?" His response: "What I think is that no one knows about this."

And that was exactly my thought, too. The idea that when we suffer, if we unite it to Christ's suffering, it can actually save souls from hell? The goal of the Holy Spirit is to reproduce Christ's suffering in us.

Wow! What a concept.

Below are some scripture verses that back this up and were mentioned earlier in this book:

Colossians 1:24: In my flesh, I complete what is lacking in Christs afflictions for the sake of the body, that is, the Church. Romans 8:16: it is the Spirit himself bearing witness with our spirit that we are children of God, and if children, then heirs, heirs of God and fellow heirs with Christ. PROVIDED WE SUFFER WITH HIM in order that we may also be glorified with him.

1 Peter 18:21: For to this you have been called, because Christ also suffered for you, leaving you and example, that you should follow in his steps.

Philippians 1:29: For it has been granted to you that for the sake of Christ you should not only BELIEVE in him, but also SUFFER for his sake.

Luke 9:23: "If anyone wishes to come after me, he must deny himself and take up his cross daily and follow me."

The Church teaches: Suffering in union with the passion of Christ…acquires a new meaning; it becomes a participation in the saving work of Jesus (CCC 1521)

Jesus' apostle John had a follower, Ignatius, who wrote very early in the Church's history:

> "If God causes you to suffer much, it is a sign that He has great designs for you and that He certainly intends to make you a saint."

St. Faustina adds:

> "Suffering is a great grace; through suffering, the soul becomes like the Savior; in suffering, love becomes crystalized; the greater the suffering, the purer the love."

Jesus speaking to Katya/Catalina Rivas:

> "A soul strengthened by suffering is like a flame that grows with the wind."

I might be a slow learner, but I finally understood. What if God cares more about the state of our souls than about our 401(k)s? What if suffering is actually a pathway that leads us back to Him? In sports, we always said, "No pain, no gain." Could that be true for our spiritual lives as well?

What if my mom's suffering, united with Christ's passion, was how my family was drawn closer to the very heart of Christ? And what if the vision I have for sharing these truths has a ripple effect—like a pebble thrown into a pond—leading thousands, or even millions, of souls to the truth of Jesus' words: "Eat My Flesh, and Drink My Blood"? Could this heal the wounds of the world caused by pride, greed, lust, envy, gluttony, sloth, and wrath—the Seven Deadly Sins?

My mom used to watch a lot of EWTN (Catholic TV). My dad? He was more into CNN, FOX, and MSNBC—always focused on the news. But now, my dad watches far more EWTN than the news channels. Since my mom's passing, his mind and heart have turned more deeply toward his faith. Don't get me wrong, my dad has always been a devoted Catholic. But now, he's picking up where Mom left off.

In the last 13 years, I've had the privilege of speaking to over 50,000 people at hundreds of parishes and conferences. I've encouraged attendees to dive into Ron's books, watch his DVDs, and read the messages of Catalina Rivas. I've helped many understand the beauty of daily Mass, praying the Mass, regular Confession, Holy Hour, and the Rosary. None of this would've happened without Christ's suffering, Catalina sharing in that suffering through the stigmata, and my mother's suffering, which ultimately led me back to the heart of worship—sacrifice, which we know as "The Mass." More on that later...

This idea that suffering is a blessing and not a curse became even clearer when I read one of Jesus' messages to Catalina about suffering:

### Jesus' message to Catalina on suffering:

"Why do you complain? The affliction you suffer, as Saint Augustine said, is a medicine, not a punishment. Job calls a man whom I correct fortunate, for I make the wound and I heal it. I hurt and I cure with My hands. I punish whom I love and test those whom I receive as My children with misfortunes (Hebrews 12:6). One day I told Saint Therese: You must know that the souls My Father loves the most are those who suffer the greatest afflictions. Learn from Job, who said: 'If we have received good things from the hand of the Lord, why should we not receive also the bad?' Do you think it is unfair that he who received with joy life, health, and riches should also receive suffering, which is more useful and beneficial than prosperity? My beloved daughter, a soul strengthened by suffering is like a flame that grows with the wind."

Reading these words from Jesus reminded me of what my mom wrote to me about a month before she suffered that heart attack while driving with Dad to Florida:

Letter from Mom, December 5, 2003:

> "There was a time when my life was all mixed up, and I was reading the book of Job to find out what the Bible had to say about suffering. I have underlined a lot of things in the Bible that spoke to me at different times. In the book of Job, I only underlined four places, but one really stood out to me. In Chapter 2, verse 10, Job had been struck with boils, and his wife said to him, 'Curse God and die.' But he replied, 'Are even you going to speak as senseless women do? We accept good things from God, and should we not also accept evil?' God does not cause evil, but He allows it for a reason. We don't always understand the reason, but we have to trust."

# Chapter 11

# Mary is Calling You

I distinctly remember coming home from my accident, where I had fallen asleep at the wheel and nearly killed myself in the early 2000s. I picked up the rosary my mother had sent me, along with instructions on how to use it. I knew I needed all the help I could get.

The word "Rosary" comes from Latin and means "a garland of roses." The rose is a symbol of the Virgin Mary. The rosary itself is a devotion focused on the lives of Christ and His mother. It's believed that honoring Mary greatly pleases her Son, Jesus. That made perfect sense to me because, just as with Jesus, if you honor my mother, you make me happy too!

The Hail Mary is a prayer straight from scripture. It ends with asking Mary to "pray for us now and at the hour of our death." Catholics see this as no different from asking a close friend or family member to pray for you. It's a beautiful expression of unity in prayer.

### A Brief History of the Rosary (from Catholic.com):

"Monks had begun to recite all 150 psalms on a regular basis. As time went on, it was felt that the lay brothers, known as the conversi, should have some form of prayer of their own. They were distinct from the choir monks, and a chief distinction was that they were illiterate. Since they couldn't read the psalms, they couldn't recite them with the monks. They needed an easily remembered prayer. The prayer first chosen was the Our Father, and, depending on circumstances, it was said either fifty or a hundred times. These conversi used rosaries to keep count, and the rosaries were known then as Paternosters ("Our Fathers").

The rosaries that originally were used to count Our Fathers came to be used during the twelfth century to count Hail Marys—or, more properly, the first half of what we now call the Hail Mary. (The second half was added some time later.)

In an article posted on www.Catholic.com, titled "The Biblical Roots of the Marian Doctrines," the question is posed, "Do You Believe Your Pastor or Martin Luther?"

It goes on to say:

> "It often comes as a surprise to Protestant fundamentalists that Martin Luther (1483-1546), the founder of the Protestant Reformation, maintained Mary was the "Mother of God" and believed in Mary's perpetual virginity and immaculate conception. Luther was a Catholic priest and monk before he decided to break from the apostolic Church. One might expect he would have rejected the Church's teachings about the Virgin Mary, but the opposite is true. Thus, Protestants are left to wiggle on the horns of a sharp dilemma. If you are a Lutheran, Methodist, Baptist, or nondenominational Christian, chances are you reject the perpetual virginity and immaculate conception of Mary. However, the very founder of Protestantism believed both of these doctrines. Should a Protestant believe his individual pastor or Martin Luther?"

In 2009, as I was praying the rosary with the "prayer ladies" (Name affectionately given to the daily Mass ladies who typically pray the Rosary before or after Mass) at St. Elizabeth Ann Seton following a daily Mass, a very pleasant lady approached me and whispered, "Can I speak to you about something?"

We walked to the front area, and she asked me what I knew about a place called "Medjugorje." The only time I had heard that name was in relation to Bob Hughes conversion story mentioned earlier. She explained to me that she had just come from staying with the visionaries in Medjugorje, the women who claimed to be receiving messages from Mary. She said that the Blessed Mother was pushing her to come and tell me what I was about to do was very important for the Church. Now, you must understand that, at this point, I have not conducted any presentations. It would be impossible for anyone to know what I was about to do because I was not even completely clear yet myself. This is a massive Church. My wife and I were brand new to the parish. There was no possibility that she would even know me. I felt like I was on a hidden camera, practical jokes show. She gave me a "Miraculous Medal" that she said was blessed by the Blessed Mother.

I decided I needed to get educated on Medjugorje. I purchased and read a book called *The Miracle Detective* by Randall Sullivan. He was a very skeptical agnostic who worked for Rolling Stone Magazine. He was an investigative journalist who wanted to find out the truth behind the claimed apparitions of The Blessed Mother. I was amazed at how deeply impacted this nonbelieving investigative journalist was after spending time in Medjugorje.

Som time later, I was attending Mass at St. Patrick's Cathedral in downtown Fort Worth, Texas. As soon as Mass ended, the lady behind me, Gerti Carpenter, whispered, "Can I speak to you out front?" We stepped to the front, and she proceeded to say, "I think our Blessed Mother is calling you to Medjugorje."

Again? Is this happening a 2nd time? I was so stunned I could barely think, much less speak.

My brain jumped from question to question in a rapid-fire sequence.

- How much would it cost?
- When should I go?
- Should I go alone?
- How will I afford this?
- How long would I stay?

One airline ticket alone would cost several thousand dollars. I would be there for a week. It's impossible! I could not leave my wife and three young children for a week and spend $5 thousand dollars.

I finally found my voice and responded, "Let me talk to my wife and get back to you."

My next shock occurred a few days later. I received an email telling me that there were people who wanted to pay for the trip for me. Elizabeth Victory, a lady I had never met, offered to pay for me to go. She said she couldn't pay for everyone but strongly felt that Mary was "calling me" there. I was very grateful for this offer, but I still thought it crazy to leave my wife and three kids for a week on such short notice.

However, I told them I would get back to them after my upcoming trip. I had scheduled a three-night presentation at a parish in Rhode Island for March 14-16, in 2011. This is a 30-hour road trip with my wife and three kids. As we pulled up to the hotel where we were staying, this billboard was displayed right there:

Pk looked at me, visibly moved, and said, "Tim, that's a sign from God—you need to go."

Not long after that, my dad surprised me by purchasing a $2,300 plane ticket and booking lodging for the week to accompany me to Medjugorje. What a blessing! I was so excited to spend this time with him.

There are no coincidences. I've written about how I believe coincidences are simply God acting anonymously, and this was one of those moments. Two different women, whom I didn't know, approached me with the same message. Another woman I didn't know offered to pay for my trip. These couldn't just be coincidences!

So, Dad and I flew to Medjugorje, a small town in southern Bosnia and Herzegovina, in what used to be Yugoslavia. The name Medjugorje means "among the mountains." We stayed in a very simple room, with no luxuries. The family we stayed with had known the three visionaries since childhood. Every day was packed from morning until night. We prayed the Rosary three times daily, fasted on Wednesdays and Fridays with only bread and water, and attended Mass daily. We also learned about the "Five Stones" the Blessed Mother gave to the visionaries:

1. Daily Prayer (15 mysteries of the Rosary)
2. Reading the Bible (Daily Scripture)
3. Eucharist (Daily Mass)
4. Fasting (Wednesdays and Fridays)
5. Monthly Confession

This trip was life-changing, and it reinforced the belief that none of this was coincidence—it was all part of God's plan.

When the decision was made to go, I wondered if I'd experience anything that could be considered "miraculous." From the moment we landed, there was an aura, a feeling, unlike anything I'd ever felt before. As it turned out, Dad and I filmed the sun dancing. It was truly an awe-inspiring moment.

During one of the apparitions, we were asked to bring forth our prayers and physically place them before the Blessed Mother, represented by a statue where she appears. As I approached her, I felt like my body went into shock. I literally started shaking and crying. But in all honesty, this could have been my imagination. I wouldn't offer my personal emotions or visions as definitive evidence of anything supernatural.

At another time, when the Blessed Mother was said to be appearing, someone in the crowd started screaming as though possessed. We were told that this reaction wasn't uncommon and that people with demons attached to them often had adverse reactions in her presence.

### Medjugorje with Dad – May 22nd – May 30th, 2011

Dad and I shared a powerful experience together in Medjugorje. In the picture, I was wearing my mom's rosary, which glows in the dark. That glow perfectly represents my mom—a light in a dark world!

In the picture, from left to right: Elizabeth, Dad, Gertie (Elizabeth was the one who paid for me to go).

My Opinion on Medjugorje is that millions of people are going to confession and receiving the body and blood of Christ there. If this is some sort of trick by the evil one, then he has surely tricked himself!

### An Offer I Couldn't Refuse

Wanting to share all of this with the world, I received an offer I couldn't turn down. Bob Hughes told me he wanted to redirect the money he was spending on newspaper advertising and instead provide it to me to promote Ron and Mike's work. This would allow me to travel across the country and present at Catholic parishes. It would cover just enough to meet our bills, and, fortunately, my wife had convinced me years ago to homeschool the kids. The idea of not missing out on time with my family, while promoting what I believed to be a solution to the brokenness and division in society, felt like the perfect opportunity.

Three other significant things happened to make this a reality. First, Fr. Jim Gigliotti, pastor of St. Maria Goretti in Arlington, Texas, read *Reason to Believe*. Dolores Sutton, the owner of Keepsakes Catholic Books & Gifts, allowed me to put up a large poster encouraging people to purchase Ron's book. Fr. Jim read the book three times and said it was one of the best books he had ever read. I reached out to him and arranged the first full two-night presentation at a parish, and the event was packed. Afterward, Fr. Jim wrote a letter to the bishop's office stating, "Attendance at daily Mass more than doubled and continues to thrive. Those attending Adoration tripled in number…"

Second, I used Fr. Jim's letter and the credibility behind *Reason to Believe* to put together a fax blast to thousands of parishes across the United States, offering presentations to boost Mass attendance. The third development came from Mike and Ron's presentation on the Blessed Mother's birthday in 2009. Bob Hughes hired a professional film crew to create a DVD titled *Science Tests Faith*, which he promoted in Catholic newspapers. Keith Kline purchased the DVD and reached out about hosting a three-night mission at St. Philip in Greenville, Rhode Island, in March of 2011.

I still laugh at the memory of Keith asking, "Can you do a three-night mission?" I responded, "What's a mission?"—which is hilarious because any devout Catholic knows exactly what a parish mission is! I was about to drive 30 hours for a three-night mission, and I had no idea what A mission was? It reminds me of St. Paul's words: "God chose the foolish things of the world to shame the wise; God chose the weak things to shame the strong" (1 Corinthians 1:27).

### Eight Months Later...

There's an old saying: "You build the airplane while you're flying it." That's exactly how it felt. Pk, our three children, and I drove 30 hours to spend three days in Rhode Island to present on supernatural events that had been tested by science. Christian was 10, Hailey was 6, and Layton was 4, and they were all excited for the road trip.

The mission was a huge success. In any mission, the attendance usually grows each day as people return, bringing their spouses and kids along for the experience.

By March 2011, my schedule was packed:

March 14-16: Greenville, Rhode Island (whole family)

March 18-20: Dubuque, Illinois (solo three-night mission)

March 22: Bowling Green, Ohio (solo one-night mission)

March 23: Reading, Ohio (solo one-night mission)

March 24: Greenville, Ohio (solo one-night mission)

While I traveled for missions, Pk drove the kids back to Ohio, making stops for American history lessons along the way. She loved the idea of teaching the kids by visiting historical landmarks in person—so much more impactful than just reading about them in textbooks. We visited New York City, Pennsylvania, and Washington, D.C., homeschooling on the go!

March 29th Philadelphia, Pennsylvania – Whole family 3-night mission

April 2nd— Saddle Brook, New Jersey— Whole family one night mission

April 12th-Back to Texas

Something else happened that month that we didn't anticipate. The engine in our Expedition stopped working, and we had to end up buying a used conversion van. The goal was to find a used van that we could pay cash for so that we could avoid having a car payment. We settled on a 1995 conversion van that said it had only 65,000 miles on it. We would find out soon enough that this was probably not true.

## Mary is Calling You

Kids washing our van as we travel the country

Kids homeschooling at one of my presentations

I had several other parish missions across the country that I handled on my own while my wife and kids stayed back in Ohio, continuing with homeschooling. The next major mission was scheduled for Colorado in September. We packed up and drove from Ohio to Colorado in our newly purchased, though older, conversion van. St. Thomas More, the largest parish in the Denver diocese, had invited us for a three-night mission from September 27th to 29th.

Brad Maddock, the event coordinator, was incredibly generous. After the mission, which drew around 700 attendees each night, Brad kindly gave us the keys to his mountain cabin so we could stay a few extra days. It was a special and unforgettable time with my family.

## Another Divine Connection

I remember a very significant phone call while we were still in the mountains after the mission at St. Thomas More.

"Tim, this is Dr. Gregory Thompson. I got your number from Bob Hughes. I know we've never met, but I lost my best speaker for a two-day conference in Glendale, Arizona. Where are you right now?"

"I just finished three nights with over a thousand Catholics in Denver, Colorado," I replied.

He asked, "Where are you going next?"

"Home," I said.

"Where's home?"

"We live in Texas, but my wife wants to stop in Arizona to visit an old friend."

"Where in Arizona?" he asked.

"Chandler," I responded.

"Would you be willing to do a two-day conference while you're there?"

"Absolutely," I replied, smiling. "I'm sure my mother and Our Lady have connected us."

What followed was a whirlwind of events that led to incredible blessings and opportunities. This was just the beginning.

"Wonderful. We'll meet at 1 PM at the parish on Saturday to go over the entire event."

I recently called Dr. Gregory to get his recollection of this series of events…

"I remember saying, 'This is how we're going to set it up for the next two days. I'm going to give Tim more of my time.' My point person, Hal Pawlowski, and our other speaker, Donald Hartley, immediately said, 'No, don't do that.' But something inside me—maybe I didn't fully understand it at the time—told me I had to. And I said, 'Yes, I'm going to do just that.' At that point, I hadn't even heard you speak, Tim, but I knew in my gut that Our Lady wanted me to make room for you.

"After you gave your first talk, I remember standing two or three inches from your face, saying, 'You are coming to my home parish.' It wasn't just a suggestion—I was certain it was a gift from Our Lady herself that she introduced you to me. I had never arranged something like this at my home parish before, but I went ahead and called Paula and John, my sister and brother-in-law. I told them, 'You have to come down and listen to this talk.' They trusted me completely, and their immediate reaction was, 'Can we have him for two days before he comes down to Marshall?' They had been in the parish for two years but had only seen a few events with about 50 people attending.

"That night, we had 200 people in attendance. By the second night, that number had grown to about 300. When you came to Marshall, we used to have one hour of Adoration each month on First Fridays. After the event, that transformed into 60 hours a week. It was amazing to witness."

## A little background on Dr. Gregory:

Dr. Gregory Thompson, a former Missouri Superintendent of Schools, faced significant challenges in his career, including being attacked by the ACLU and fired on Mary's birthday, September 8, 2004, simply for acknowledging God in schools. He served as President of the Ozark Schools Superintendents and Missouri State Chairman of the Sportsmanship Committee, which he helped establish for the state of Missouri. The children affectionately called him "Mr. T," and he lived by the values he instilled in them, putting up banners in the schools that read: "Stand up for what is right even if you stand alone," and "Do what is right even if no one is watching." Dr. Gregory also ran for Governor of Missouri in 2008.

Over the past twelve years, he has organized twenty-seven Marian conferences, always striving to be more like Mary, keeping himself grounded by adding her name to his own. His deep desire to bring souls to Jesus through Mary is inspiring. Thanks to his efforts and influence, I've had the privilege of presenting more parish missions in Missouri than in any other state. I've never met anyone more devoted to the Catholic Faith than Dr. Gregory.

Dr. Gregory Thompson

Here's a picture from a presentation I gave at St. James in Glendale, Arizona, thanks to Dr. Gregory. My family stands alongside Pastor, Hal and his wife:

One of my favorite quotes about the miraculous comes from G.K. Chesterton:

"The believers in miracles accept them (rightly or wrongly) because they have evidence for them. The disbelievers in miracles deny them (rightly or wrongly) because they have a doctrine against them."

Having promoted Ron & Mike's work for over 13 years, I've found Chesterton's quote to be absolutely true. Every "skeptic" I've encountered comes with a presupposition that "miracles don't happen" or that "Jesus is a made-up story." None of their critiques are ever based on real evidence. When presented with overwhelming facts, their responses tend to be along the lines of "they must have cut themselves" or "it's just the power of the brain."

St. Padre Pio, for example, was accused of manifesting the wounds of Christ due to his excessive concentration on the Passion. His response? I love it. He said, "Go out to the fields and look very closely at a bull. Concentrate on him with all your might and see if you start to grow horns."

It's high time the world accepts that supernatural occurrences like Stigmata, Eucharistic Miracles, statues crying and bleeding, and incorruptible bodies of saints are real. And not just from the past — these things happen even today. Instead of being closed-minded, we should focus on learning the context of these miracles and understanding the message behind them. More on that later.

## A Blind Priest, An Enormous Inspiration

Through my dear friend Dr. Gregory, I've had the fortune of connecting with many parishes in Missouri. After finishing a presentation in Springfield, Missouri, I was introduced to Fr. Coon, who I later found out is legally blind. His story deeply inspired me, and I feel compelled to share more about this remarkable man.

Fr. Coon was so enthusiastic about the Eucharistic Miracles I presented that he immediately invited me to speak at his church, St. John's, in Leopold, Missouri. Spending time with Fr. Coon is an incredible experience because he treasures conversations. He listens with such attentiveness, absorbing every detail of what's said. His lack of physical sight seems to have enhanced his ability to listen — he's one of the greatest listeners I've ever known. Attending Mass with him, watching him slowly and joyfully pray the Mass in Braille, is like witnessing someone savoring an exquisite meal. His passion for the faith is contagious, and I encourage everyone, regardless of their beliefs, to attend one of his Masses. Fr. Coon currently serves as the Pastor of Sacred Heart in Dexter, Missouri.

Raised in Charleston, Missouri, Fr. Coon is the youngest of seven boys. His father was a devout Catholic, and his mother joined the Church after they married, though she was raised in a devout Baptist home. Fr. Coon was born on December 1, 1965. By the time he was six months old, his parents noticed that he wasn't responding to light the way his older siblings had. They took him to a local doctor, who initially thought it might be a brain issue. However, after further evaluation at Cardinal Glennon Hospital in St. Louis, it was discovered that he had been born with congenital cataracts. He endured several eye surgeries from the age of six months until he was fifteen.

Earlier in my memoir, I mentioned how I believe coincidences are "God choosing to act anonymously." Fr. Coon's story is another example of that. He was baptized as an infant on December 13, which just so happens to be the feast day of St. Lucy, the patron saint of the blind. He says this is a clear demonstration of God's providence. He was also confirmed on December 13. Another coincidence?

Fr. Coon's parents sought a second opinion from another ophthalmologist to ensure everything that could be done was being done. This doctor found some blockage that could be removed, and on June 18, 1981, he underwent a special surgery. As a result, he has no vision in his right eye but limited sight in his left.

In 1972, as a first-grader, his parents made the difficult decision to send him two and a half hours away to the state school for the blind. They wanted to give him every chance at independence, but imagine driving that far to drop off your youngest of seven children, just starting first grade, to live among strangers.

He attended the school for the blind through fourth grade, learning Braille and essential skills for navigating a sighted world. He returned to Charleston in fifth grade to attend the local Catholic school, St. Henry. He remained there through eighth grade, then moved on to high school in Cape Girardeau. Other students helped him take tests by reading questions and writing down his answers. He commuted 40 miles each way to attend high school, where he was elected President of the Student Council in his senior year. His campaign slogan? "A vote for Coon is a vote for experience."

I've always been curious about what led him to the priesthood. He told me that, beginning in the fifth grade when he became an altar server, the idea of priesthood had been growing in him. His family never missed Mass, and he started to think about becoming a priest very early on.

His mother, fondly known as "Mama Coon," encouraged him to be a lector in seventh grade. She would read Bible verses aloud to him, and he would transcribe them into Braille so he could read them at the ambo.

During his senior year of high school, in June 1984, his father asked him to make a decision about his future. He told his dad he wanted to enter seminary and become a priest. His parents were fully supportive.

Even though no seminary had ever trained someone who was legally blind before, he was accepted into Conception Seminary College, run by the Benedictines in Conception, Missouri. He studied there for four years.

Curious how he managed to succeed? His Baptist grandmother spent those years recording all his theology books onto cassette tapes. "My Baptist grandmother helped to make a priest for Jesus," he told me with a smile.

When Fr. Coon was ordained on May 30, 1993, the bishop jokingly announced at the reception that he would give Fr. Coon's Baptist grandmother an honorary degree in

Catholic theology for all the recordings she had made for him.

Being legally blind helped Fr. Coon hear the call to priesthood. It gave him deeper compassion for those who suffer, and it has made him more humble, aware of his own need for God, and empathetic to the struggles of others.

When I asked him recently, "What's the greatest treasure you've received as a Catholic priest?" he answered without hesitation, "Celebrating the Holy Mass."

I've prayed many Masses with Fr. Coon, and it's like watching someone savor a dessert with their eyes closed, enjoying every bite. For Fr. Coon, being the instrument through which God unites Himself with His people is the greatest joy of his priesthood.

Jesus said, "If you eat my flesh and drink my blood, I live in you, and you live in me."

Fr. Coon's story reminds me of what Jesus said in John 9:1-3:

"As He passed by, He saw a man blind from birth. And His disciples asked Him, 'Rabbi, who sinned, this man or his parents, that he was born blind?' Jesus answered, 'It was not that this man sinned, or his parents, but that the works of God might be made manifest in him.'"

Fr. Coon holding Romeo

It's been one of the greatest joys of my life getting to know this holy man, someone who has become a dear and beloved friend.

### One More Challenge

Our eight-month road trip came to an abrupt end with a family crisis. We had been renting a house while we were looking for a place to buy. There was a verbal agreement with the owner that we'd extend our rental for another year. But just when we were expecting to finalize the lease, the owner lost his job in California and needed to move back to Texas. He needed his house and, without much notice, we learned he wouldn't be renewing the lease.

Moving is always a challenge, but when it's unexpected, it becomes even more difficult. Throw in homeschooling, traveling, and life on the road, and the situation was quickly becoming overwhelming. Pk and I are very different when it comes to handling our "stuff." I'm quick to throw things out if we don't use them regularly, whereas she prefers to keep just about everything. This situation, paired with the sudden need to move, was a recipe for stress.

But as always, Pk rose to the occasion. She found a new rental—a four-bedroom, 3,000-square-foot home for only $1,100 per month, which was saving us hundreds of dollars. We went into high gear, packing, loading, and getting everything ready. We managed to move into the new house, and at first, it seemed like a blessing in disguise. The neighborhood was full of kids playing, and the rent was too good to be true. And, in a way, it was.

Eight months flew by, filled with parish missions, homeschooling, and sports. I was coaching the kids in basketball, baseball, and football, and life was a whirlwind. I was away on a trip when Pk called with some unbelievable news.

"You're not going to believe what just happened," she said.

"Great," I responded, already bracing for impact.

"We have thirty days to move out again!"

I was speechless. A woman had knocked on the door and asked Pk what she was doing living in her friend's house. You can imagine Pk's confusion. We had a signed lease and had been paying rent for eight months. As it turned out, the person we signed the lease with was a scam artist. This person had been breaking into foreclosed homes, changing the locks, and leasing them out at unbelievably low prices. We had been conned, and now, once again, we had to move at a moment's notice.

The time, money, and emotional energy spent moving twice in less than a year were enough to test the strongest of families. We had plenty of turmoil—housing, money, schooling, you name it. But by God's grace, through the regular reception of the Eucharist—His body, blood, soul, and divinity—we managed to stay strong and weather the storm.

And just when we thought the storm had passed, another challenge appeared on the horizon. During a mission trip to Colorado, the air conditioning in our van broke down. The cost to fix it was higher than what we paid for the van itself. We finally decided to purchase a new Expedition, complete with a full warranty. As nice as the new vehicle was, I will forever cherish the memories made in that old 1995 conversion van. Traveling across the country with the whole family, from Rhode Island to California, those were some of the best times of my life. The simple things, like a pool and a breakfast bar at a Holiday Inn or Comfort Inn, were all we needed to feel like royalty.

The greatest blessing I've received from God in promoting His work has been the endless hours spent with my wife and children on this journey. Another blessing has been the many trips I convinced my dad to come along for. Dad is easy to please—give him a hot breakfast, coffee, a warm shower, an afternoon nap, and he's happy. Growing up with eleven siblings on a farm, living simply was second nature to him.

For years, I had prayed for more time with Mom and Dad, realizing that living in Texas made regular visits difficult. Looking back now, I can see how God answered those prayers. Dad and I spent countless hours traveling to parish missions together, sharing meals with people who deeply care about their faith. One common thread among many of them is the distress they feel because their children and grandchildren no longer practice the Catholic faith.

As for more time with my mother, that prayer was answered by my spiritual mother. Below is an excerpt from Catalina Rivas's messages, describing a vision she had during Holy Mass:

> Catalina Rivas: "There began to appear in front of the altar some shadows in human form, gray in color, and they were raising their hands upwards.
>
> The Holy Virgin said: 'These are the blessed souls of Purgatory who wait for your prayers to be refreshed. Do not stop praying for them. They pray for you, but they cannot pray for themselves. It is you who have to pray for the blessed souls in order to help them depart [from Purgatory], that they may go to their encounter with God and enjoy Him eternally.'
>
> Catalina Rivas: 'The moment of Consecration had arrived, the moment of the most marvelous of Miracles... Behind the right side of the Archbishop appeared a multitude of people also in a diagonal line. They were dressed in the same kind of tunics as the Guardian Angels but in soft colors: rose, green, light blue, lilac, yellow; that is, in different and very soft colors. Their faces were also brilliant, full of joy. They all seemed to be of the same age. You could tell (and I cannot say why) that there were people of different ages, but their faces looked the same,

without wrinkles, happy. They all knelt down as well, at the singing of the "Holy, Holy, Holy Lord…'

Our Lady said: 'These are all the Saints and the Blessed in Heaven, and among them are also the souls of your relatives and family members who already enjoy the Presence of God.'"

This experience brought me great peace, reminding me of the power of prayer and the closeness of those we love, even after they've passed. God's grace truly sustains us in every storm.

Chapter 12

# The Ordinary Activity of the Devil

My brother Mike, who has always been my biggest supporter through both the good and bad times, organized a talk for me at St. John Neumann in Sunbury, Ohio. I spoke on the first two nights, and Fr. Vincent Lampert took the stage on the third night. Fr. Vincent is currently the pastor of two parishes and has been the exorcist for the Archdiocese of Indianapolis since 2005. Anytime someone mentions stigmata, exorcism, Eucharistic miracles, or anything supernatural, I'm all in! So, I sat in the front row, taking notes on everything Fr. Vincent said. Two topics stood out the most.

The first was what Fr. Vincent called "The Ordinary Activity of the Devil." He stressed that most of us will never experience the "Extraordinary Activity of the Devil," where the devil uses infestation, vexation, obsession, or possession as his tools. Instead, we need to be aware of how the devil attacks us in our everyday lives. He explained that evil rarely shows up looking like evil; it comes quietly and subtly. He got very specific about the devil's tactics, and I love specifics. I thought of it like coaching football: if I could study the Michigan Wolverines' game plan against Ohio State, I'd have a better chance of beating them.

As I mentioned earlier, my mother wrote to me saying, "You are not wrestling with flesh and blood but against principalities and powers." She was quoting Paul's letter to the Ephesians. So, keeping in mind that I didn't want to lose this battle and become a slave to sin, I took notes as if my life depended on it.

Fr. Vincent explained that the devil uses a four-stage plan to attack us. I call them "The 4 D's":

1. Deception: This leads to...
2. Division, which leads to...
3. Diversion, and ultimately ends in...
4. Discouragement.

If you think about it, all division—whether in personal relationships, in our country, or in the world—starts because someone feels deceived. Deception always leads to division. And where there is division, we find people being diverted away from virtue and into vice. This downward spiral leads to discouragement.

Fr. Vincent also explained that in the world of diversion, we replace God with ourselves, following three guiding principles:

1. You may do as you wish.
2. No one has the right to command you.
3. You are a god of yourself.

When people are caught up in chronic sin, they often fall into discouragement, leading to depression, anxiety, and in some cases, suicide. Fr. Vincent noted how anxiety, depression, and suicide are now epidemic among teenagers.

## The Ordinary Activity of the Devil

I remember one powerful thing Fr. Vincent said: "The devil hasn't upped his game. Rather, more people are showing a willingness to play his game."

The second topic that really caught my attention was the eight major ways people create entry points for evil to enter their lives. I'll share five of them here and relate them to how I, too, opened doors to evil:

1. **The World of the Occult:** In college, I dabbled in this by conjuring a spirit while on acid and visiting a psychic who read my palm. These things are more popular now than ever.

2. **The Entertainment Industry:** I've watched many shows and movies that promote vice instead of virtue. Growing up, we watched wholesome shows like Little House on the Prairie and The Waltons. Later, we ended up with shows like Sex and the City. Now, soft porn is on regular TV.

3. **Abuse:** I'll touch on this in a bit.

4. **A Life of Habitual Sin:** Fr. Vincent pointed out that humans have always struggled with sin and find delight in things like alcohol, drugs, pornography, and promiscuity. Alcohol and drug addiction nearly destroyed my life.

5. **Unhealed Broken Relationships:** You've probably heard, "I'll forgive, but I won't forget," or "I could never forgive them." The Lord's Prayer asks God to "forgive us our trespasses as we forgive others."

It's one thing to highlight problems, but Fr. Vincent also gave solutions—"best practices to fend off the devil." To show you how wise my mother was, I've included excerpts from letters and journals she wrote over 25-30 years ago next to each of Fr. Vincent's recommendations:

- **Read and know the Bible:** Mom said, "I have underlined a lot of things in the Bible that have spoken to me at different times."

- **Practice Marian Devotion:** "I'm sending you a rosary booklet. I am becoming more and more aware of the strength I've received from praying the rosary, especially when I pray for others."

- **Frequent the Sacraments:** "He touches us in the sacraments (all seven of them), and He comes to us physically in the Eucharist. Please consider beginning your healing process by going to confession. It's a very healing sacrament. Don't forget St. Michael the Archangel."

- **Pray and fast:** "I've started fasting on Wednesdays and Fridays for our children and their special needs."

- **Call upon your Guardian Angel:** "Every morning, say a morning offering, a prayer to your Guardian Angel, and a prayer to St. Michael. Use your Guardian Angel and holy water. This is a spiritual battle—be on your guard."

- **Use Sacramentals:** "Pray at least a decade of the rosary every day. Bless yourself everyday with holy water. I will do that in the morning for all of you. I name each of you and sprinkle holy water."

Mom's wisdom continues to amaze me. Jesus said, "Blessed are the poor in spirit," meaning those with humility. My mother was the humblest person I've ever known. The greatest blessing God gave her was seeing her family practicing the Catholic faith. After my talks, people often come up to me and say, "Your mother must be so proud of you." I always respond, "I work for my mom—both my mother and Our Blessed Mother." Mom is working from the other side with Our Lady, the saints, and my Guardian Angel to guide us to eternal life. Thank you, Mom. I love you.

## Why be Catholic With all the Sexual Abuse?

Two weeks after Fr. Vincent's talk, I found myself sitting down for breakfast with another exorcist priest at a conference in Boston. The first morning, I asked him to share his story, and I was stunned as it unfolded. He had been molested by a priest at a young age, even in his own home with his parents present. The priest made him believe his parents approved of it—deception at its worst.

By the time he was old enough, he had left the Church and his family behind. He became a very successful investment banker, rubbing shoulders with people like Brad Pitt and George Clooney. But his life spiraled into alcohol, drugs, and sexual immorality, leading him to despair. His turning point came in Medjugorje, where he had a powerful conversion experience. At almost 50 years old, he became a priest and now serves as an exorcist in the U.S.

Let me answer the question, "Why be a Catholic with all the sexual abuse?" by sharing Jesus' words to Catalina Rivas:

> "How many priests and Bishops who thought they were wise, are in Hell today! How low they have been brought by their arrogance. Pray, My little daughter. Make amends for the offenses and the insults I receive from many of My consecrated ones..."

Jesus' message is clear: Regardless of your role in life, if you destroy the innocence of another, you will be dealt with severely by God.

The Bible quotes Jesus as saying, "Whoever causes one of these little ones who believe in me to sin, it would be better for him to have a great millstone hung around his neck and to be drowned in the depths of the sea" (Matthew 18:6).

Why would someone molested by a priest choose to become one? It's the same reason someone abused by a coach or teacher might become a dedicated coach or teacher: they believe in what the position offers. There are bad people in every organization, and the Church is no different. A Catholic priest is necessary for the bread and wine to become the Body and Blood of Jesus Christ. Without them, we cannot receive Jesus in the Eucharist. More on this in the next chapter.

# Chapter 13

# God's Solution to Fighting Evil

Another question that someone might ask, is "Why would someone want to eat Jesus' flesh, and drink his blood?

Jesus was as clear as He could possibly have been when he said:

- I am the Living Bread sent down from heaven. He who eats my flesh and drinks my blood shall not die but will have eternal life. (John 6:51)

- He who eats my flesh and drinks my blood has eternal life and I will raise him up on the last day. (John 6:54)

- He who eats my flesh and drinks my blood abides in me, and I in him. (John 6:54)

The biblical, historical, and supernatural evidence showed me that only by attending a Catholic Mass can anyone receive the Eucharist (eat Jesus' flesh and drink His blood).

- The Apostle John's disciple Ignatius wrote: "Take care, then, to use one Eucharist, so that whatever you do, you do according to God: For there is one flesh of our Lord Jesus Christ, and one cup in the union of his blood; one altar, as there is one Bishop, with the presbytery and my fellow servants, the deacons."

- Catalina Rivas, the woman who received the stigmata and was filmed at that time (as seen on the show Signs from God-Science Tests Faith), received this message from Jesus: "I have said: 'This is My Body,' and this statement carries the force of My Omnipotence if it is proclaimed by My authentic Ministers."

- Jesus' "authentic ministers" would be those to whom he gave the gift and responsibility of consecrating the bread and wine to the Eucharist and then passing it on to others. To determine who is specifically authorized to consecrate the bread and wine to the Eucharist, we simply need to determine what Church Jesus founded.

| Church | Founder | Year Founded |
|---|---|---|
| Calvary Church | Chuck Smith | 1965 |
| Mormon Church | Joseph Smith | 1830 |
| Disciples of Christ | Thomas Campbell | 1809 |
| Baptist Church | John Smyth | 1609 |
| Presbyterian Church | John Knox | 1560 |
| Calvinist Church | John Calvin | 1536 |
| Anglican Church | King Henry VIII | 1534 |
| Lutheran Church | Martin Luther | 1517 |
| Eastern Orthodox Church | Eastern Patriarchs | 1054 |
| **Catholic Church** | **Jesus Christ** | **33** |

## The Demons Believe and Tremble

I was introduced to a man who had worshipped the devil for 26 years. One day, a woman handed him a Miraculous Medal and said, "The Blessed Mother is calling you into her army." Zachary, not knowing who the Blessed Mother was, took the medal in his hand, and immediately, everything went dark. The woman then began telling him things about his life that she could not have known—about a dark ritual he had performed the night before, assisting in over 100 abortions—and she repeatedly said, "That was of the devil."

For a deeper dive into Zachary's incredible conversion, search for:

> "Top Satanist's ASTONISHING Miraculous Medal Conversion w/ Zachary King."

Zachary shared something else with me that truly startled me:

> Satanic covens pay people up to $5,000 for a consecrated host from a Catholic Mass. Why? Because as Scripture says, "Even the demons believe—and tremble." (James 2:19)

Demons believe in God; they just refuse to follow Him. They hate His ways. Satanic groups know what happens during a Catholic Mass. On one group's website, they openly describe a "Black Mass" as a perversion of the Catholic Mass, where a consecrated host is desecrated to mock Christ.

I don't mean to be offensive to non-Catholic Christians, but it's significant that Satanists don't break into non-Catholic churches to steal crackers and grape juice for their Black Masses. They know the power of the Eucharist, and that's why they go after consecrated hosts.

Another former Satanist, Betty Brennan, who also converted, said, "If we had a bona fide witch here with 2,000 hosts, and only one was consecrated, that witch would know immediately which one it was."

You can find Betty's full story by searching "Former Satanist Becomes Catholic."

For me, this is more evidence that affirms the ancient belief that Jesus is truly present in the Eucharist. Even those involved with the demonic world understand the truth of the consecration.

## Common Objections to the Catholic Church

As other Christian denominations have formed over the centuries, some common objections have been raised against the Catholic Church. Here are a few with responses:

> **Objection:** The Catholic Church became corrupted, so God had to create new denominations.
>
> **Answer:** When Jesus changed Simon's name to Peter, meaning "rock," He said, "Blessed are you, Simon Bar-Jona! For flesh and blood has not revealed this to you, but my Father who is in heaven. And I tell you, you are Peter, and upon this rock I will build my Church, and the powers of death shall not prevail against it. I will give you the keys of the kingdom of heaven, and whatever you bind on earth shall be bound in heaven, and whatever you loose on earth shall be loosed in heaven." (Matthew 16:17-19). If the Church became corrupted, then the gates of hell would have prevailed, which goes against what Jesus promised.
>
> John's disciple Ignatius in the second century said, "It is possible, then, for everyone in every Church, who may wish to know the truth, to contemplate the tradition of the apostles which has been made known to us throughout the whole world. And we are in a position to enumerate those who were instituted Bishops by the apostles and their successors down to our own times. Follow the Bishop, even as Jesus Christ does the Father, and the presbytery (or priests) as you would the apostles; and reverence the deacons as being the institution of God. Let no man do anything connected with the Church without the Bishop."
>
> St. Augustine, in 397 A.D., said:

"There are many other things which most properly can keep me in [the Catholic Church's] bosom. The succession of priests, from the very seed of the apostle Peter, to whom the Lord, after his resurrection, gave the charge of feeding his sheep [John 21:15–17], up to the present episcopate, keeps me here."

## To summarize why a person molested by a priest would become a priest:

- The historical evidence supports the belief that Jesus Christ existed, was crucified, and rose from the dead.

- The historical evidence supports the belief that we can trust the New Testament documents.

- The historical evidence shows that Jesus established a Church that would be the "pillar and foundation of truth."

- The Church that Jesus established, along with the Saints and Mystics, has always taught the necessity of Priests administering the Sacraments to feed Jesus' sheep, especially "eating his body and blood" in the Eucharist.

- A few bad apples in any organization does not mean that all the apples are bad. There are evil people in every organization. If Jesus is a real person from history who died for our sins and rose from the dead, then we should follow "the pillar of the foundation of truth" that he established (1 Timothy 3:15).

- If you are going to follow what he taught, wouldn't it make sense to read what the followers closest to him and his apostles said that he taught?

As quoted in Stephen Ray's book *Crossing the Tiber:*

"Who would understand the teachings of Christ

and the apostles more accurately: those who knew them and the generations immediately following, or those living two thousand years later? Who would have a better grasp of the language, the tradition, the religious milieu, and the spiritual teachings and practices: people today, many of whom have cut themselves off from the anchor of history, or those who suffered and died for their faith, with the "apostles" teaching still ringing in their ears"? (Stephen Ray, *Crossing the Tiber*, Page 170)

As quoted earlier, the famous convert to the Catholic Church, John Henry Cardinal Newman, stated clearly, "To be deep in history is to cease to be Protestant."

He also said the following:

"I betake myself to one of our altars to receive the Blessed Eucharist; I have no doubt whatever on my mind about the Gift which that Sacrament contains; I confess to myself my belief, and I go through the steps on which it assured me. The presence of Christ is here, for it follows upon Consecration, and Consecration is the prerogative of Priests. Priests are made by Ordination, and Ordination comes in a direct line from the Apostles. Whatever be our other misfortunes, every link in our chain is safe; we have the Apostolic Succession, we have a right form of consecration: therefore, we are blessed with the great GIFT."

There is virtually no doubt that the Church leaders in the early centuries after Christ's resurrection passionately believed in the Eucharist.

St. Ignatius called it "the medicine of immortality."

St. Irenaeus said, "Our flesh becomes incorrupt, and partakes of life, and has the hope of resurrection," as "being nourished from our Lord's body and blood;" that the Eucharist "is made up of two things, earthly and heavenly."

Origen and Magnes, after him, say that the Eucharist is not a type of our Lord's Body, but is His Body, and St. Cyprian uses language as fearful as can be spoken of those who profane it. I cast my lot with them, I believe as they.

## The Healing of Souls Creates an End to Division

Our country, the world itself, as well as many families are divided. Many leaders believe that we, as people, are as divided as at any time in history. Recall that division is the goal of evil spirits. By the power of my mother's prayers, I was led to the remedy to heal division, fight evil, and heal my soul. Here is a recap of the ancient spiritual medicine that saints, mystics, exorcists, and prayer ladies like my mom have used to bring about peace for themselves and those they love:

## The Word of God

"When you received the word of God which you heard from us, you accepted it not as the word of men but as what it really is, the word of God, which is at work in you believers" (1 Thess. 2:13).

> "Stand firm and hold to the traditions which you were taught by us, either by word of mouth or by letter" (2 Thess. 2:15).

Sacred Tradition and Sacred Scripture together form the deposit of faith, guided by the Holy Spirit within the Church.

"Ignorance of Scripture is ignorance of Christ." (St. Jerome)

"The Word of God is the most effective tool that we can use to defeat the devil. Jesus used it to renounce the temptations of the devil at the beginning of his public ministry, and in doing so, teaches us to do the same."
-Fr. Vincent Lampert— Exorcist for the Archdiocese of Indianapolis.

## Confession (Reconciliation)

Jesus told the apostles, "As the Father has sent me, even so I send you.' And when he had said this, he breathed on them and said to them, 'Receive the Holy Spirit. If you forgive the sins of any, they are forgiven; if you retain the sins of any, they are retained" (John 20:21–23).

"Confession is the soul's bath. You must go at least once a week. I do not want souls to stay away from Confession for more than a week. Even a clean and unoccupied room gathers dust; return after a week, and you will see that it needs dusting again!"
—Padre Pio quote-who suffered the stigmata for fifty years:

Confession supernaturally heals a soul in the same way that proper medicine heals wounds. As Jesus said to

the stigmatist Catalina regarding Confession to a Priest: "It is a medicine for the soul. Vices are cured. Temptations are repelled. The stalking of Satan is destroyed. New grace is acquired. Virtues grow."
— Jesus to Catalina Rivas. The mystic and stigmatist

"Confession is more powerful than exorcism. One is a Sacrament, and the other is a blessing. The devil wants to destroy the soul, and the soul is healed by Confession. One Confession is worth 100 exorcisms. If people want to decrease the work of Satan, they should increase the use of Confession."
—Fr. Gabriela Amorth (Exorcist for the Diocese of Rome)

"Talk to the world about Sacramental Confession, that source of saving water that awaits everybody, and whoever is immersed in this water will be protected from the enemies of the soul."
—Jesus to Catalina Rivas

"When you go to Confession, to this fountain of mercy, the Blood and Water which came forth from my Heart always flows down upon your soul."
— Jesus to St. Faustina— The mystic and stigmatist

"Confession heals, Confession justifies, Confession grants pardon of sin. All hope consists in Confession: in Confession, there is a chance for mercy."
— St. Isidore

### Connecting Confession to the Mass

Jesus, speaking to Catalina, said, "When those filthy and repugnant hands dealt Me blows and slaps, I saw how often I would be struck and slapped by so many souls who, without purifying themselves of their sins, without cleaning their house with a good CONFESSION, would receive Me in their hearts."

The Apostle Paul said: "Whoever, therefore, eats the bread or drinks the cup of the Lord in an unworthy manner will be guilty of profaning the body and blood of the Lord." And anyone who eats and drinks without discerning the body eats and drinks judgment upon himself."

This is why the Church that Jesus established teaches:

> "Anyone conscious of a grave sin must receive the Sacrament of Reconciliation before coming to Communion." (CCC 1385)

Oil and water do not mix. You cannot put something perfectly holy (Jesus Christ) into a soul that has been severed from Christ through grave sin. This is why having confession before every Mass makes perfect sense to me.

### The Catholic Mass

"Unless you eat the flesh of the Son of Man and drink his blood, you have no life in you."  -Jesus Christ (John 6:53)

"The Heart gives life; a body cannot live without it. In the same way, the heart that gives life to the Church is the Holy Mass.
— Jesus to Catalina Rivas. The mystic and stigmatist

"Through the diligence in hearing Mass, you will obtain corporal and spiritual blessings: preservation from many misfortunes; and strength against temptations which would otherwise have vanquished you. The best help you can afford the sick, suffering, and dying is to hear Mass for them."
— Venerable Martin von Cochem

"If men only appreciated the value of the Holy Mass, they would need traffic officers at Church doors every day to keep the crowds in order."
— St. Padre Pio

"Holy Communion preserves and increases the supernatural life of your soul. It maintains, increases, and repairs your spiritual forces."
— Fr. Lawrence Lovasik

"The Eucharist is a <u>daily Bread</u> that we take as a remedy for the frailty we suffer daily."
— St. Augustine

"Receive Communion often, very often… there, you have the sole remedy if you want to be cured. Jesus has not put this attraction in your heart for nothing."
— St. Therese of Lisieux

"Holy Communion is the shortest and safest way to Heaven."
— Saint Pius X

### Holy Hour/Adoration of the Blessed Sacrament

"Adoration outside of the Holy Mass prolongs and intensifies all that takes place during the Mass."
— His Holiness Benedict XVI

"Through ADORATION, the Christian mysteriously contributes to the radical transformation of the world."
— Saint John Paul the Great

"Even though most of the time you are not aware of it, you leave those encounters with a renewed energy and increased strength to face life with all its sufferings."
— Jesus to Catalina Rivas. The mystic and stigmatist

"Do not let so many useless worries pull you away; reserve a moment of your time to visit the Prisoner of Love. If your body is sick, can you not find a few minutes to look for a physician to cure you? Come to Him who can give you the strength and health of the soul."
— Jesus to Catalina Rivas. The mystic and stigmatist

"Jesus has made Himself the Bread of Life to give us life. Night and day, He is there. If you really want to grow in love, come back to the Eucharist, come back to that Adoration."
— Saint Mother Teresa

"I know I would not be able to work one week if it were not for that continual force coming from Jesus in the Blessed Sacrament."
— Saint Mother Teresa

"What will convert America and save the World? My answer is prayer. What we need is for every parish to come before Jesus in the Blessed Sacrament in the Holy Hours of Prayer. Every Holy Hour we make will so please the Heart of Jesus that it will be recorded in Heaven and retold for all eternity."   — Saint Mother Teresa

### Prayer, the Mass, and the Blessed Mother

"The Holy Mass is a prayer itself, even the highest prayer that exists. It is the Sacrifice, dedicated by our Redeemer at the Cross, and repeated every day on the Altar."
— Saint Pius X

"No prayers offered for your friends will be as efficacious as a single Mass heard and offered on their behalf."
— Venerable Martin von Cochem

"The Blessed Mother is a powerful ally for anyone who is up against the forces of evil. The devil could not touch the Blessed Mother because she was full of Grace."
-Fr. Vincent Lampert—Exorcist for the Archdiocese of Indianapolis

"When you pray the Rosary for someone, every bead is a drop of My blood, and those drops fall on the person for whom it is offered."
— Jesus to Catalina Rivas. The mystic and stigmatist

"If families give Our Lady fifteen minutes a day by reciting the Rosary, I assure them that their homes will become, by God's grace, peaceful places."
-Father Patrick Peyton

"The Rosary is a powerful weapon to put the demons to flight."
— Pius XI

"Some people are so foolish that they think they can go through life without the help of the Blessed Mother. Love the Madonna and pray the rosary, for her rosary is the weapon against the evils of the world today. All graces given by God pass through the Blessed Mother."
—St. Padre Pio

"The Rosary is a sort of machine gun and atomic bomb, namely, a weapon that is far superior to all the weapons of modern warfare in overcoming the enemy of God."
—Servant of God Joseph Kentenich

### What is the point of the Mass?

A popular priest with two very popular podcasts called "The Bible in a Year" and "The Catechism in a Year," by the name of Fr. Mike Schmitz, made this statement, "...the point of the Mass is not to receive Holy Communion..."

This statement always shocks Catholics when I show this quote at my presentations.

Most Catholics, including those who go to Daily Mass, believe that the main reason to go to Mass is to receive Holy Communion. Receiving Holy Communion and being able to eat Jesus's flesh and drink his blood is an amazing gift. However, as Fr. Mike says:

> "...the point of Mass is to offer the sacrifice of the Son of God to the Father."

> "...there is one priesthood of Christ, but two different 'participation' in the one priesthood."

Jesus Christ is on the altar at every Mass, offering his once-for-all sacrifice to the Father. He is not dying again. The same sacrifice is represented in an unbloody manner. The ministerial priest is the one with the white collar on the altar. We in the pews, as baptized Catholics, are "kingdom priests."

The bottom line is that we are obligated to offer the Son of God to the Father with the ministerial priest. In fact, Fr. Lawrence Lovasik says, "The measure of profit you draw from the Mass is the measure in which you offer yourself in union with Christ."

Fr. Mike Schmitz says it perfectly: "The heart of worship is not singing a song. It is not saying a prayer. No, the heart of worship is sacrifice. The place of sacrifice is an altar."

GOD'S SOLUTION TO FIGHTING EVIL

This is a perfect visual:

In his book *Come to the Altar*, Fr. Mike Schmitz sets the stage for how Jesus wants us to worship:

> "Jews throughout Israel would travel with families to Jerusalem for the Passover. They would carry a lamb around their shoulders so that it did not get hurt. They would take an unblemished lamb that was precious to them and bring it to the Temple. They would present the lamb to the priests as a sacrifice to the Lord, and the priests would collect its blood and

> pour it onto the altar. The family would then take the lamb home and consume it. At the Temple, the sacrifice of the lamb was completed when the blood was poured out on the altar. At the Last Supper, Jesus is saying, 'This is my blood poured out.' And then he commands his disciples, "Do this in memory of me.' In these powerful words, Jesus makes it absolutely clear how He wants us to worship him. Offer up the sacrifice. Offer up me, once for all, blood poured out, body given over."

Many feel that if they do not get a great message from the Mass, they have not been "fed" spiritual food. This is not the point of the Mass.

As Fr. Martin von Cochem tells us, "The Holy Mass is not a sermon, it is not intended for the instruction of the people; it is the offering for them of the Sacrifice of the New Testament."

Fr. Mike Schmitz sums everything up perfectly: "My prayer is that no Catholic will ever show up to Mass and just watch. My prayer is that they will never just show up to Mass and waste their kingdom priesthood, but instead, they will intentionally offer the sacrifice of the Son to the Father with the ministerial priest. The HEART of worship is sacrifice, not whether we get something from it or whether we are entertained. We are not here to watch or be entertained. We're here to offer up the sacrifice of the Son to the Father in the power of the Holy Spirit."

When we offer Jesus and ourselves through praying the Mass, we help in the salvation of the world. Could you imagine being at the foot of the cross where Jesus was hanging after being scourged, whipped, beaten, nailed, and stabbed? Standing there looking up and saying, "I am not being fed here. I prefer something a little more entertaining."

This is precisely what my dad was saying when he said

the non-denominational Church was all about entertainment. My dad was not formally educated. He knew nothing about theology. But he is wise. He was saying exactly what Fr. Mike Schmitz was saying now. The Mass is a sacrifice. Being crucified and hung on a cross is not meant to be entertaining. Mass should not be "fun." As I typed these words, my son and I just finished our last two days of football practice together. Two a day is not meant to be fun. It is a sacrifice that increases virtue in the boys and helps produce character. It helps turn a boy into a man. The Mass provides "supernatural spinach" to help us win the spiritual battle. After all, those who persevere to the end will be saved.

## Dennis Kirkpatrick

On August 17$^{th}$ 2018, I received an email from Michelle DiEnno. It read:

> "Please help us save our parish, OUR LADY OF FATIMA in Secane, Pa. I know if you come here, you will help bring many young people back to Christ. Watching your videos changed my life, and I would love to give that gift to so many who have lost their FAITH. Tell me where to start. We need a spark in our community, and I believe you are it. A dear friend from Church gave me your video Signs by God and it gave myself, my sister, and my cousin a whole new perspective on the sacrifice of the Mass. Since then, we have gone to Mass and adoration daily as if it were our job. A man named Dennis, who shared your video with us, has since passed away. I know he would be so excited to know you came to Our Lady of FATIMA to help save souls like he did, always promoting your videos. He also was on a mission sharing your videos with men in a halfway house to bring them back to Christ through Our

> Most Blessed Mother. We are in desperate need of Resurrection in our Parish Community. The young people are not coming to Church. I truly believe they just don't understand the miracles that happen in the Holy Sacrifice of the Mass. You have a special way of conveying it so that the laity comprehends it. Please help us save souls and fill our Church again with the zeal for Our God. May God continue to Bless you and use you to bring his children back."

Prior to getting this email from Michelle, I had been communicating with Dennis Kilpatrick at the same Church for several years. He had contacted me via email after watching my DVD *Signs from God — Miracles and Their Meaning*. He desperately wanted me to come to his parish and present and do my presentation. I always felt like I was talking to Rocky Balboa. He was, in fact, an avid boxer. He could never get the staff at his parish to cooperate with organizing me to come. This is the norm. Dennis was going through cancer. Michelle had ended up with him in a morning rosary group.

He gave Michelle my DVD, *Signs from God*. She told me she cried through the whole thing. Dennis passed away on February 17th, 2017.

During three days in October 2019, Michelle, along with a group of prayer warriors, hosted my family at Our Lady of Perpetual Help in Morton, PA. It was a packed house all three nights. The Pastor, Msgr. John Savinski wrote a letter of reference following the three nights that included these comments:

> "Tim's presentation was quite overwhelming, to say the least, and he was extremely well received. The presentations drew close to 1000 people from 55 parishes across the Archdiocese of Philadelphia.

> I highly recommend Tim Francis and his Signs from God-Science Tests Faith to other pastors and parishes, especially in this age of so much confusion and indifference to many of the essential truths of our Catholic faith."

Crazy! This rebellious, irresponsible drug addict named Tim Francis got prayed back into the Catholic faith by a devout mother. He then got filmed, and that DVD reached a guy in Philadelphia. Before he died, he handed Michelle the DVD. Two years after getting the DVD, my whole family came to Our Lady of Perpetual Help and close to 1000 people got to hear the message that Dennis Kirkpatrick so desperately wanted to bring to the area. No doubt, Dennis Kirkpatrick & Patricia Ann Francis were working on the other side to orchestrate this!

I was blessed to have a woman named Geraldine Miller come to the presentation. Providentially, her confirmation name is my mother's name, Patricia Ann.

In Geraldine's own words after attending the presentation:

> "It was early August when the doubts regarding the truth of Holy Eucharist crept into my thoughts. On this particular day, August 3, 1994, I was attending morning Mass. It was during the Liturgy of the Eucharist that my doubts filled my thoughts. In my thoughts, I asked, 'Jesus, are you really there? I can hardly believe you're a piece of bread.' At the moment the bells of Consecration rang out, I looked up, and the Church was filled with a brilliant light. it was Jesus standing in the priest's hands, with his heart exposed and dripping blood toward the chalice on the altar. I knew at that moment that Jesus is really and truly fully present in the Most Blessed

From The Crack House to God's House

Sacrament. I also knew the image needed to be shared."

The" Bread of Life" image is an artist's rendering of a vision sketched by Geraldine Miller and described in more detail to her. It depicts the moment of transubstantiation during the consecration of the Holy Sacrifice of the Mass. This beautiful image not only inspires us all but, more importantly, confirms the absolute truth of the Read Presence of our Lord Jesus Christ in the Eucharist.

Go to www.EucharisticJesus.org for full details fn this story. There you can download an 8" x 10" print of the *Bread of Life* painting.

Geraldine next to the image

## My Mother

"If one of your loved ones is far away from us, pray for him. Give him to My Mother, and She will bring him in Her arms to Me."

— Jesus to Catalina Rivas. The mystic and stigmatist

This is a photo of my mother in Lake Tahoe right after Pk and I were married outside of the Catholic faith. She is asking Jesus' Mother to bring me back to the Catholic faith. This "coincidentally" happened on the Feast of the Assumption of Mary. August 15th.

Just to be clear, I am not Catholic because my mother wanted me to be Catholic. I investigated the claims of the Catholic Church to honor my mother's request to "search for the truth." It used to be that if you grew up Buddhist, you would be Buddhist. If you grew up Baptist, you would be Baptist. While there are certainly "cultural" or "cradle" Catholics, Atheists, Mormons, etc., more and more people are questioning why they believe what they believe. My dad's generation seemed to have a high regard for authority and didn't seem to question much. That can be both positive and negative. I didn't want to follow something that would restrict my freedom just because I was brought up with that belief. I certainly have better things to do with my time than going to daily Mass if this was all a product of my parents buying into a fairytale. However, the historical and supernatural evidence for this being true is overwhelming!

My Mother was the humblest, kindhearted woman you could ever meet. Looking back through her letters and diary, she has proved to be the wisest of all. If you could speak to my mother, I know what her "life advice" would be. By God's grace, I still have her letters.

Here are some primary takeaways from letters my mother wrote to me leading up to her death:

**1999**—"If you can't find a Catholic Church that has Adoration of the Blessed Sacrament, go to weekday Mass and spend some time afterward with your reading, your prayers, your silence. Don't receive the Eucharist unless you really believe it is the Body of Christ and unless you go to Confession."

**2001**— My primary prayer for all of you is that you know the Lord and he guides your life.

**2002**— Begin each day with prayer. Make that a priority in whatever you do. SEEK THE KINGDOM OF GOD FIRST in all you do.

**2003**—Remember to begin each day with prayer. If the Church is open, go sometime and spend some time in front of the Blessed Sacrament, giving the Lord your problems. Go to daily Mass if you can.

I am eternally grateful that I was able to tell Mom how much I appreciated her years before she died. Below is a letter I wrote to her for Mother's Day while I was living in Texas. I hope you won't wait to share your feelings with those you love.

**Dear Mom,**

I hardly know where to begin. There are so many things that have gone unsaid over the years. I should be ashamed of myself. I am so proud that you are my mother. I have tears streaming down my face as I try to put into words how much love and appreciation I have for you. Everything you and Dad could give; you always gave to the family. You have always put other people's needs ahead of your own. You always call me or send a letter at just the right time in my life. You have no idea how many times I've been down and needed a loving hand, and suddenly I heard from you. Thank you for coming to all our baseball games and making peanut butter and jelly sandwiches for everyone afterward. Thank you for taking the time to pray for the family and for keeping God close by. Thank you for always making everybody feel welcome in our home. Thank you for always cooking dinner, doing laundry, and making sure that everybody was happy. I realize that this may sound a little scattered, but I'm just typing as my thoughts come to me. I really regret not being able to spend more time with everybody in the family. Days just seem to fly by. I've been very homesick lately. I miss everybody so much!! It's so nice to have so many great childhood memories to think back to. Pk and I rented *Jesus of Nazareth* a few days ago and spent the weekend watching it. It reminded me of how you used to make cookies and watch this will all the family. Mom, those memories are invaluable. You are and have always been everything that I could have asked for in a mother. My relationship with God has never been stronger in my life. I am certain that God kept his hands close to me during my recent low times because of your constant love and prayers. I'm sorry that I haven't thanked you enough for your constant unwavering love and support throughout the years. You have always been there for me, and I'll never be able to tell you enough how much I love you!!!

**REMEMBERING...**

Remember the games,
Remember the fun,
I'll never forget you walking back and forth
Only to miss Mike and I hitting home runs.

There was always a schedule
And a designated plan.
Regardless of the outcome,
Mom was our number one fan.

It was late to bed
And early to rise
I appreciated the pre-made oatmeal
But the warmed donuts were a huge surprise.

## God's Solution to Fighting Evil

Setting the table
And then washing the dish
Deciding which book to bring
Cause she's not the one who wants to fish.

Always unselfish
Providing for the team
Heck, Phil didn't like cold cereal
So she made him some wheat and cream.

Remembering my mom
How could I forget?
She's the whole reason
That God and I met.

Mom laid the foundation
To be morally correct
If there was a president for mothers
It should be my mom we elect.

Remembering my mom
Brings nothing but joy
Happy Mother's Day mom
From your second to youngest little boy.

Thank you for being my mother. I love you!

PS: You always encouraged me to write like Dr. Seuss, so I thought I'd give it a try.

Love, Tim

I believe with my whole heart and soul that I would not be doing what I'm doing today, would not be married to the love of my life, and would not have the three beautiful children I've been blessed with without the "power of my mother's prayers", both when she graced the earth and after her passing from Heaven. I firmly believe that she's working in partnership with our Blessed Mother to begin to heal the world, one person at a time. The picture below is Mom and me in early 2000.

# About the Author

Tim Francis is a nationally known speaker/evangelist and founder of You Shall Believe Ministries in Fort Worth, Texas. After years of addiction, he was thrust into a search for truth after witnessing a lady experience the stigmata, the wounds of Christ. Discovering centuries-old scientifically documented miracles and supernatural happenings, he set out on a quest in 2009 to share these findings with the world.

As the father of three children and has been married for twenty-five years, Francis travels the United States today, putting on multimedia presentations that show the biblical, historical, and supernatural evidence of Jesus Christ's teachings and practices up until today. He is currently working on a major motion picture, inspired by true events, of a priest & exorcist who was abused by a priest as a child and became a self-absorbed Wall Street banker before having a riveting conversion that led him back to Christ's church to serve as both a Pastor and Exorcist.

Here is sampling of thousands of testimonials after attending his presentations and/or watching videos:

"I wanted to thank you for changing my life. My mom went to day 1 of the 3-day mission… she got me to attend the second day… I was an occasional Mass attendee, mostly holidays. After your talk I made a good confession and now attend Mass DAILY…."

"I thank you from my heart for the 3 days of 'Science Tests Faith'… Because of ignorance, I was bringing pain to Jesus just as those who beat and crucified Him. No more!! After over 40 years, I received the Sacrament of Confession again, and will continue from now on…I am so fired up to do as much as I can for Jesus and to spread what I've experienced."

"Without hesitation, nor exaggeration, I can say it was this presentation that was the pinnacle of my return to the Catholic Church…Two days after the event, my 10 year old daughter asked if we were going to start going to the Catholic Church. I told her, I think so, but did she understand that…they taught that the bread and wine actually become the body and blood of Jesus Christ. Without hesitation she stated, 'Well they do, remember, we saw the video.'..In that moment, through the eyes of a child, I was given clarity of purpose and my family and I returned to the Catholic Church."

"My wife noticed the video "Science Test Faith" in the back of St. Mary's several days ago… Over the past 73 hours, I feel as though I have undergone a religious transformation. Once you watch the video… there is no going back. As a doctor, I consider myself a scientist of sorts… (who) utilizes evidence-based clinical decision making whenever possible. You and your colleagues are providing an awesome service… truly life-altering and, I think, ultimately soul saving. Thank you very much and God bless you all!"

You can reach Tim at
www.ScienceTestsFaith.com
francis.tim13@gmail.com
866-671-7284